Rebound From Burnout

Resilience Skills for Ministers

Third Edition

The Living Well Series, Volume 3

The Living Well Series

Volume 1: *Finishing Well: Retirement Skills for Ministers*
Ministers face much more difficult retirement issues than most secular individuals. They not only lose their occupation, but they often lose friends, culture, identity, self-esteem and too frequently, even their future hope of effective ministry. This book addresses:

- What is a successful retirement for a minister?
- How can you know when it is time to retire as a minister?
- How can you gracefully transition to a new ministry?
- How can you survive and even thrive like never before?

Volume 2: *Transforming Conflict: Relationship Skills for Ministers*
Filled with real-life examples from ministry, this handbook provides research-proven skills that help ministers prevent relationship discord and strengthen ministry relationships. This book helps ministers learn:

- How to prevent and eliminate relationship obstacles
- How to cultivate research-proven relationship skills
- How to adapt each of the relationship skills to their ministry

Volume 3: *Rebound From Burnout: Resilience Skills for Ministers*

Volume 4: *Transforming Personality: Spiritual Formation and the Five-Factor Model*
Using the spiritual disciplines and personality assessment tools, this book equips Christians with skills that build intimacy with God, and opens their personality to grow more like Him. The reader learns how to interpret the Five-Factor Personality Model to assess personality factors and facets, fruit of the Spirit, motivational gifts of the Spirit, ministry aptitudes, vocational aptitudes, and preferred styles of behaviors.

Rebound From Burnout

Resilience Skills for Ministers

Third Edition
The Living Well Series, Volume 3

Nathan Davis

Beth Davis, D.Min.

Cover photo and chapter photos by iStockphoto.

Third Edition

ISBN-13: 978-1475217643
ISBN-1475217641

Printed in USA

Dedication

To Edith Davis

 A resilient lifestyle characterized Grandmother Davis. Although she lived well before the advent of most resilience and burnout research, she innately knew how to transform hardship and suffering into resilience.

She survived her first major setback in the 1940s when a doctor diagnosed one of her sons with tuberculosis—an almost certain death sentence at that time since a tuberculosis antibiotic did not yet exist. Five years later, her eldest son died in an automobile accident. When her husband died of a heart attack soon afterward, she began the daunting task of raising her remaining five children, alone. She suffered a fourth set-back when a daughter died unexpectedly. Grandmother Davis also faced three life-threatening cancer surgeries. Each time, she rebounded from suffering with yet more grace and beauty.

After her 70th birthday, she decided to learn a new skill—to play the piano. And she succeeded in teaching herself!

Years after her death at age 92, friends and former Sunday school students continue to point to Edith Davis as their spiritual mentor. In addition to her Sunday school students, she mentored her family. Upon salvation, her son with tuberculosis received instantaneous healing and subsequently served 48 years as a foreign missionary. Another son and grandson served as ministers. And two other grandchildren continue to serve as foreign missionaries.

Edith Davis rebounded again and again from hardship and suffering. Perhaps because of hardship and suffering, her life influenced more individuals than anyone this author knows.

Table of Contents

PART I:

Ministers Need

Resilience

CHAPTER 1

What Is Burnout and Resilience?

Three approaches

Two villages existed on opposite sides of a steep and treacherous mountain and each village engaged in commerce with the other. As individuals struggled to transport goods between the villages, every now then one of them slipped on the steep mountainside and sustained serious injury. A missionary passing through noticed the problem and suggested a solution—plan #1. He offered to purchase an ambulance to transport the injured victims to the nearest hospital, about four hours away. The villagers felt overjoyed and the missionary bought them the ambulance. The ambulance cost $40,000.

However, after a few years the ambulance needed repairs. The villagers complained that they couldn't afford the repairs. And since the missionary had already returned to his home country, no financial help came from him. While the ambulance lingered in disrepair, several villagers fell and needed hospitalization. So the villagers asked a new missionary to help.

The new missionary suggested a new solution—plan #2. He suggested building them a clinic at the foot of the mountain. Injured villagers could obtain medical help readily without the need of an ambulance. He easily raised the construction funds and obtained a work team from his home country to build the clinic. Within a few months, they finished. A second team trained local personnel with basic medical skills to operate the clinic. The building cost $120,000. The short-term trips to build it and train the local personnel cost $35,000.

However, the villagers found that the local staff never received adequate training for the more serious injuries, and medical supplies never seemed available or affordable. Worse yet, with their new skills the staff found that they could obtain higher paying jobs in the capital of the country. Without any ongoing medical training for replacement staff, the medical staff gradually dwindled away. Within a few years, the clinic had to close for lack of medical staff. The villagers complained.

Tired of hearing complaints, a local villager suggested a new solution—plan #3. He had considered mentioning the plan when the first missionary arrived, but the local villagers seemed so excited about getting a free ambulance that they never seemed open to consider anything else. So the man with plan #3 had remained quiet about his proposal. However, he still believed that his plan might work—he suggested that the villagers build guard rails along the mountain pathways to prevent the falls. Without anyone else available to offer help, the villagers agreed to try his approach. With a little effort, they cut trees from their local forest, split rails and posts for the guard rails, and installed them. Since they used local labor and local resources, they could easily maintain and repair the guard rails. The guard rails cost the villagers less than $100 for cement to set the posts. No one needed the clinic any longer, so they used the facility to raise pigs for the village (The above story was adapted from a presentation at a Community Health Evangelism (CHE) seminar at AGWM HealthCare Ministries in April 2012).

Exercise 1-1: Like plan #1, some church agencies routinely bring burned out pastors and missionaries to a Christian-based clinic in their home country. What are some direct and indirect costs associated with this approach for just one family in your agency? If an average of 40% of pastors and missionaries suffer from burnout over their career, what are some potential direct and indirect costs associated with this approach for your agency over the next ten years?

In some countries, local churches implement a similar approach—they send their ministers to a Christian counseling clinic that serves their entire denomination. Within your denomination and setting, who represents the participants in a solution similar to plan #1?

Exercise 1-2: Like plan #2, some church agencies run local clinics to provide more accessible clinical services to burned out pastors. Instead of sending pastors to a clinic in distant location, some local pastors cross train into the counseling profession to help other pastors within their own region or area. What are some direct and indirect costs associated with this approach? If an average of 40% of pastors suffer from burnout over their career, what are some potential direct and indirect costs associated with this approach for your agency over the next ten years?

Some local churches implement a similar approach—they operate a local counseling center to help burned out ministers. Within your agency and setting, who represents the participants in a solution similar to plan #2?

Exercise 1-3: Some readers tend to focus on the relative cost of plan #1, #2, and #3. Is cost the most important issue? What is the most important issue? (Hint—what remained as the most important issue in the story, above?) After comparing different insights from several individuals, see page 226 for a possible answer.

Expectations

Using the above examples, this book represents the approach used by plan #3. Resilience skills serve as the guard rails in plan #3. By implementing the research completed since 1999 at least 90% of burnout and clinical depression now remains preventable. And some psychologists argue that all burnout now remains preventable. Resilience training represents a sustainable approach to counteract burnout. By using the most recently developed technology, ministers can almost always prevent burnout even while increasing their effectiveness. And with resilience skills, those individuals affected by burnout can rebound much more quickly, usually without a need for counseling or any other medical help. Resilience may never look as glamorous as a new ambulance or medical clinic, but prevention offers the most cost-effective and most successful approach to enhance minister longevity and effectiveness.

Counselors will always remain in demand—too often for those who fail to develop and maintain resilience.

When you finish reading this book, you will be able to refine:
- Research-proven skills that stimulate physical resilience (a margin of physical hardiness that prevents depression and a downcast spirit).
- Research-proven skills that stimulate emotional resilience.
- Bible-based lifestyles that stimulate spiritual resilience.

Exercise 1-4: Jeren Rowell (2010) reports that nearly 40 percent (39.8%) of currently active pastors that he surveyed have considered leaving vocational ministry during the past three years. Which of the above plans, #1, #2, or #3 best describes the approach to sustain ministers in your church or agency? What can your church and agency do to better promote their resilience skills?

What is resilience?

We define resilience as the *capacity* of an individual to cope positively with stress and negative events such as crises. Resilience includes:

1. The *ability to rebound* to a "new normal" that represents a healthy condition after a negative event (a stressor).
2. *Adaptability* that uses a stressor to build additional hardiness against burnout.

This book provides resilience skills for ministers to prevent and recover from burnout. For ministers (and especially missionaries and chaplains), stress remains fundamentally different from secular individuals. Due to the unforeseen and unpreventable stress and crises brought by their church members and others in their community, most ministers experience five to ten times more stress than secular individuals. While secular individuals may survive with little margin of resilience, few ministers avoid burnout (long term exhaustion) unless they develop skills that promote resilience.

Three resilience support legs provide the *ability to rebound*:

1. Physical resilience
2. Emotional resilience
3. Spiritual resilience

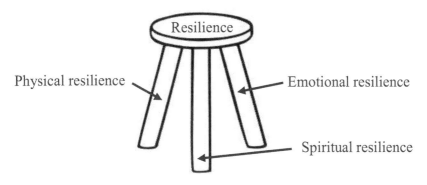

Adaptability characterizes all three leg stools. That is, a three leg stool inherently provides the ability to adapt to jagged or shifting ground.

Most ministers spend a considerable amount of time developing spiritual resilience, but correspondingly less time developing physical and emotional resilience. However, a weakness in any single leg can cause the stool to collapse. Burnout occurs with the breakage of any single support leg.

The capacity for resilience seems comparable to the capacity of three cups of water that represent physical, emotional and spiritual resilience. Every cup provides a capacity to store a liquid. However, from a distance, no one can see if the cup is full, half-full, or empty. Likewise, most individuals cannot see their level of physical, emotional or spiritual resilience. They assume that they possess adequate resilience for any stress coming their way, but rarely notice their dwindling resources for the three types of resilience until they suddenly discover one of their resilience cups dry. Without an ability to notice the level of their resilience, they feel shocked to find themselves burned out and unable to rebound. Thus, resilience tends to dwindle so insidiously that few ministers recognize their shortfall until burnout suddenly disables them.

What is burnout?

Traditionally, burnout refers to a rocket that burns fuel as it climbs into the sky. Engineers try to design the rocket to avoid burnout (burning out of fuel) until it reaches the intended altitude goal. Like a rocket in burnout, some individuals burn out before reaching their goals. Like a rocket that exhausts its supply of fuel, they simply cannot function any longer.

For ministers, "burnout" represents a North American term that describes long-term exhaustion and inadequate resilience. For many cultures, however, the term "burnout" poses a problem. I (Nathan) recently returned from Tajikistan, where I asked about the frequency of "burnout." After a rather puzzled look from my interpreter, she explained that they never use the term "burnout." Instead, they and many other cultures use, "downcast in spirit," or "poor in spirit" to describe the Western concept of burnout or depression. The terms "burnout" or "clinical depression" only emerged in Western cultures with the advent of modern medicine in the 1900s. Although Western cultures use the terms "depression" and "burnout" to describe long-term exhaustion, many other cultures never use these terms. Instead of a single word, they describe the condition as "poor in spirit," or sometimes refer to the "downcast in spirit." Jesus says, "Blessed are the poor in spirit, for theirs is the kingdom of heaven (Matthew 5:3)." Psalm 34:18 refers to the "crushed in spirit." Without a comparable word for depression, Psalm 38:6-8 uses descriptive narrative to describe the same condition, "I am utterly bowed down and prostrate; all day long I go around mourning. For my loins are filled with burning, and there is no soundness in my flesh. I am utterly spent and crushed; I groan because of the tumult of my heart." This description by King David certainly sounds like a major depression. Psalm 102:4 further describes the essence of his depression, "My heart is stricken and withered like grass; I am too wasted to eat my bread." Coincidentally, a change in appetite acts as one of the key symptoms to burnout and depression. Psalm 41:6 uses the same words as my Tajik interpreter when it says, "My soul is cast down within me." In Psalm 42:3, King David asks, "Why are you cast down, O my soul, and why are you disquieted within me?" Modern cultures invent the terms "burnout" or "depression" as near synonyms for the biblical descriptions, "downcast in spirit" or "poor in spirit." And this book also uses "burnout" and "depression" as synonyms for "downcast in spirit" or "poor in spirit."

Burnout in ministry remains fundamentally different than burnout in a secular occupation. In a secular occupation, most stress remains somewhat manageable (hence the abundance of books offering stress management skills). However, a normal ministry lifestyle includes at least five times more stress and 100-500 times more crises than what the average secular individual experiences. Each minister not only experiences his or her own crises, but also the crises of everyone else in their congregation and greater community. And the minister feels much more affected than the causal observer of a crisis. Usually, the minister knows the individual in crisis well, and grieves over the crisis like everyone else in the immediate family. When the crises of others weigh down a minister, we say that he or she suffers from "compassion fatigue." However, compassion fatigue merely represents burnout caused by ministry to those in a crisis. And almost all the church member crises remain inherently unmanageable for the minister. Since a minister cannot manage the stress of another individual, stress management rarely works in ministry. Therefore, this book avoids conventional stress management approaches. Instead, it focuses on a vastly different set of research (prevention related studies) completed since 1999. Most importantly, this book applies the research to the unique vocation (calling) of ministry.

Successive stressful events and crises lead some ministers to gradually experience depression and a downcast spirit. However, a few ministers seem to rebound relatively quickly and even develop additional resistance (resilience) to stress. This book focuses on the skills and behaviors of those in the latter group—those who recover quickly and develop additional resilience. Ministers (especially foreign missionaries and chaplains) need resilience. To a large extent, it defines their ability to remain productive in a chronically stressful vocation.

CHAPTER 2

Why Ministers
Need Resilience

True confession

Brian (not his real name) seemed perplexed when he sent me an email about feeling depressed, especially since he had written his master's degree thesis on stress management. He carefully analyzed each new task to lighten his workload. Now, his workload seemed unrealistically light—he even felt guilty for delegating almost everything to a local colleague. With so little work, what kept stimulating his downcast spirit? Regardless how much he tried to reduce his workload and responsibilities, his spirit felt chronically downcast. He entered a deep depression in which he received an ultimatum: resign from his ministry agency or get terminated. He resigned.

A chronic downcast spirit represents the opposite of resilience. At least half of ministers suffer from a downcast spirit sometime during their career. A downcast spirit results primarily from two sources. First, some individuals work too long without a rest. For these folks, they simply need rest and a behavioral change. For them, prevention and

11

recovery requires stress management to prevent overwork.

Because many secular individuals work too long without a rest, they assume that overwork causes burnout among ministers. Although overwork characterizes many ministers, other factors stimulate their burnout more than overwork. This was the case for Brian.

The second and most prevalent source of a downcast spirit for ministers results from environmental stressors. These stressors remain mostly outside of their control, and therefore respond little to stress management skills. For instance, King David experienced intense outside stress when King Saul pursued him into the desert. The stress induced by King Saul remained totally outside of David's control. And with those stressors totally outside his control, stress management principles could never help him. Like King David's flight from King Saul, most stressors in ministry remain totally outside the minister's control.

A downcast spirit results from insufficient resilience. And, burnout and a downcast spirit are types of depression.

Like most ministers, Brian suffered from this second source of stress. He couldn't figure out why his stress management skills failed. By the time Brian asked for help, he had transferred almost all of his workload to co-workers. Yet, two months later, he entered a deep depression. Many sources stimulate depression, and the environmental stressors common to ministry serve as the leading cause of a downcast spirit (burnout). Although burnout may or may not result from environmental factors, burnout always results in depression.

Brian entered a two-year bout with depression. He (along with his friends) blamed himself for failing to manage stress. Although Brian felt abnormal, his feelings were entirely normal. His environment, however, remained extremely abnormal.

What causes stress for ministers?

Holmes and Rahe (1967) published a well-known study on stress. They derived a stress scale (standardized from 1 to 100 with 100 representing the highest level of stress possible for any single event). By averaging perceptions between thousands of individuals, they found that the events of life commonly induce the following stress levels:

EVENT	Level	EVENT	Level
Death of spouse	100	Mortgage > 2.5 X income	31
Divorce	73	Foreclosure	30
Marital separation	65	**Change in work functions**	**29**
Jail	63	Child leaving home	29
Death of a family member	63	In-law troubles	29
Personal illness/injury	53	**Outstanding achievement**	**28**
Marriage	50	**Starting/quitting school**	**26**
Fired from work	47	**Wife starting/quitting work**	**26**
Retirement	45	**Changed living conditions**	**25**
Family illness/injury	44	**Revised personal habits**	**24**
Pregnancy	40	Troubles with boss	23
Sexual problems	39	**Change in residence**	**20**
New family member	39	**Change in working hours**	**20**
Business readjustment	**39**	**Change in schools**	**20**
Change in financial state	**38**	**Change in recreation habits**	**19**
Death of a close friend	37	**Change in church activities**	**19**
Change in spouse arguments	35	**Change in social activities**	**18**

By summing the scores for each event that occurred *during the past twelve months* you can determine his or her average stress level. Some of the above stressors relate to traumatic events while others relate to lifestyle transitions. Please note that the events highlighted in bold represent stresses induced by transition to a new church assignment or into a status as a foreign missionary. By summing the events shown in bold, you will note that the average newly assigned minister or first-term missionary experiences about 326 units of stress due to transition to the field of his or her calling. After completing language school, missionaries usually transition to a new location and experience all these transition stressors for a second time within their first term. In contrast, the average North American lives year-to-year with a score of about 100 from all factors, combined.

Holmes and Rahe found the following in their research:

- Those with a score between 150 to 199 have a 37 percent chance of minor illness in the next two years.
- Those with a score between 200 to 299 have a 52 percent chance of minor illness in the next two years.
- Those with a score over 300 have a 79 percent chance of major illness within the next two years.

Thus, transition to any new ministry assignment (and especially to an overseas assignment), may cause an unhealthy stress level. However, the Holmes and Rahe scale accounts only for events common in the everyday North American culture. It fails to account for environmental and cultural stressors common to ministry in many parts of the world. For instance, other highly stressful events (especially in less developed countries) that ministers sometimes face include:

- A chronic lack of security
- Driving hazards
- Isolation
- Culture shock
- Assaults on self-esteem

Foreign missionaries also get to experience the stress of language school. Each of these six chronic environmental and cultural stressors is roughly equivalent to the 29 units of stress brought by a "change in work functions" shown in the above chart. Thus, the average minister arrives to his or her new assignment with approximately 326 units of stress from transition. In some cultures, the six unique environmental and cultural factors above can add another 174 units of stress for a combined total of 500 units of stress.

In addition to the transition stressors and environmental/cultural stressors, some ministers (especially missionaries and ministers in many third world countries) also experience crises that are unique but common to their culture. These crises include events such as:

> Severe auto accidents—now tied with armed robbery as the leading cause of death for missionaries worldwide
>
> Armed robbery—especially common throughout Latin America, Africa, Eurasia, and Eastern Europe
>
> Assault
>
> Car-jacking—especially common throughout Latin America, Africa, Eurasia, and Eastern Europe
>
> Kidnapping—common in Latin America and Africa
>
> Civil war and insurrection—almost a norm in much of Africa
>
> Natural disasters
>
> Expulsion—always a problem in sensitive countries, but now common even in Western Europe

When any of these crises threaten personal death, it is roughly equivalent to the 53 units of stress brought by a "personal illness or injury." When any of these crises threaten your spouse or children, it is roughly equivalent to the 44 units of stress brought by a "family illness or injury." However, intentional man-made stressors confer the most damage. For a man-made crisis, jail time (at 63 units of stress) represents a more equivalent level of stress.

A single act of expulsion (either expulsion as a missionary from a country or expulsion as a pastor from a church) usually produces enormous stress. Initially, it seems equivalent to being fired from work (47 units). Unlike a secular individual who loses his or her job, however, an evicted missionary or minister also experiences all the transition stressors (another 174 units of stress) upon expulsion. Missionaries and pastors who change fields or churches involuntarily attest to the devastating effect of that event. Expulsion due to political decisions within a country confers a severe effect—about 221 units of stress (174+47). However, expulsion due to decisions by agency or local church leadership confers an even more devastating effect. Since this rejection occurs "within the family," it seems more similar to a divorce than the loss of one's job. Sometimes, an expulsion offers the best choice for everyone. Unfortunately, expulsion usually occurs at the end of a long history of escalating stressors (stressors similar in effect to in-law troubles and trouble with one's boss) that along with expulsion and transition can easily put the minister within reach of a major illness. When a minister needs to change fields due to disagreements with co-workers, we recommend rest and recuperation along with relationship skill training (see *Transforming Conflict: Relationship Skills for Ministers*, listed on page ii of this book).

With any decline in the economy, most ministers face a daunting financial crisis. And this crisis remains mostly outside of their control. Many ministers find that their financial support drops 25 to 50 percent during a recession. When a North American church member loses his or her job, they can file for unemployment and receive up to 24 months of government aid for retraining. When a minister or missionary loses monthly support, few options remain. Some ministers get secular jobs, and some missionaries give up their career status for an associate status or forgo major portions of their normal budget. Regardless, the financial stress affects self-esteem and sometimes translates into chronic stress.

However, the most common source of minister stress remains the least recognized—vicarious exposure to others in crisis including poverty, death, and illness. Simply witnessing church members and others in crisis stimulates large amounts of unrecognized stress that can, by itself, induce burnout and depression. In North America, the average secular individual may witness one or two incidences of severe crisis, death, or life-threatening illness during a lifetime. In most churches and in some third-world cultures, crises, poverty, death, and life-threatening illness seems like a daily obstacle course. Each instance of vicarious stress brought by church and community members adds 29-39 units of stress, depending on the depth of the minister's friendship and intervention. The cumulative effect of living as a pastor to those in chronic crises, poverty, death, or life-threatening illness often induces severe helplessness related stress. However, most ministers cannot remain as voyeurs of those in their community or congregation. Like Jesus, they get personally involved with those in crisis. Thus in any single year, many ministers experience 200-300 units of stress from this source alone. And this source of stress remains chronic year after year, and remains almost totally unmanageable. That is, no minister can prevent a crisis in the family of his or her parishioners. For most ministers, a call into pastoral care inherently represents a call into chronically high levels of mostly unmanageable stress.

When discussing units of stress in the range of 500-600 units, the exact level of stress seems relatively unimportant—anything over 300 remains extremely unhealthy.

Some insights about ministerial stress come to mind:

- Almost all the stress discussed above remains outside the control of the minister. That is, ministerial life inherently includes the transitions shown in bold as well as the environmental stressors unique to each culture and ministry. These remain mostly unavoidable occupational hazards.
- A normal minister lifestyle sometimes includes inherently unhealthy levels of stress.
- Recovery from stress levels over 300 units of stress (transition and environmental stressors) usually takes at least two years. By this time, a host of new stressors may have appeared.

Exercise 2-1: Look at the events in your life *over the past twelve months*.

- Compile your stress score from the Holmes-Rahe chart listed above.
- Add the additional stress from any of the applicable environmental and culture factors listed above.
- Add the additional stress from your exposure to crises in your adopted culture.
- Add the additional stress from exposure to individuals in crisis, including poverty, death, and illness.
- What is the sum of all your stresses?

Note that the higher the dose (the number of exposures to crisis), the more damaging the effect. Consider the following:

1. As a general rule, by the third crisis, an individual grows four times more susceptible to burnout or depression.
2. At any point in time, about 40 percent of North Americans need only one additional crisis to induce burnout.

For ministers who departed from their previous assignment due to a church or personal crisis, they will almost certainly arrive at their new assignment with minimal margin against burnout. Some ministers arrive on a new assignment with two or three crises in their recent past (such as conflict with a prior church board or staff). As they experience the additional transition stressors, environmental stressors, and crises common to their new culture, the symptoms of burnout or depression seem inevitable. Their colleagues sometimes wonder why a minister burns out so quickly, when in fact he arrived at his assignment with minimal margin (resilience) against stress.

The authors routinely talk to individuals who feel as if they can barely survive as a minister after spending several years with a Holmes-Rahe score over 500. No wonder they feel burned out.

Some church pastors experience a crisis every week through the experiences of their church members. Since the higher the dose, the more damaging the effect, many ministers and missionaries successfully survive the stressors over the first three to five years only to exceed their stress margin and finally succumb to stress during the next few years. Suffering from depression (a downcast spirit), their productivity falters, their relationships blow up, or they quit altogether.

Reflect on the number of your coworkers who burned out over the past ten years. For some, their burnout follows as a normal result of their stressful environment, regardless of their workload or stress management skills. Contemplate for a moment, will it help these ministers to hear: "Suck it up," or "Manage your stress better," or "Go to the hardware store, buy a ladder, and get over it?"

A downcast spirit rarely results as a failure of the minister—it usually results as a normal by-product of the minister's stressful environment and occupation.

Ministers sometimes feel abnormal due to burnout. However, the stressors remain abnormal, not the minister. That is, a downcast spirit occurs as normal result for anyone living with more than 300 units of stress. The stressors inherent to ministerial life remain mostly uncontrollable. Because of environmentally induced stressors, ministers rarely need stress management skills—they primarily need skills to build more resilience.

However, God continually calls ministers to serve dysfunctional people. The call into ministry leads almost every minister into harm's way.

How can I assess burnout and depression?

Hundreds of events and conditions induce depression. Burnout serves as only one of many causes. However, the symptoms of depression remain the same regardless the source. According to the American Psychological Association, depression represents a depressed mood with four or more of the following (SPACEGIS) symptoms:

S—sleep disturbance (insomnia or hypersomnia)

P—psychomotor retardation/agitation

A—appetite change or weight change

C—concentration difficulty, such as difficulty in making decisions

E—energy loss

G—guilt or excessive worthlessness

I—interest or pleasure in usual activities is lessened or lost

S—suicidal thoughts

Of all these symptoms, ministers seem particularly sensitive to guilt. Some ministers feel guilty for failing to win enough converts. Some missionaries in sensitive countries feel guilty for concealing their calling and restricting their evangelism, even while they feel guilty for risking expulsion whenever they engage in evangelism efforts. They feel guilty if they do, and guilty if they don't. Thus, some ministers deal with chronic inappropriate guilt. If it were appropriate guilt, they would readily ask forgiveness and get on with their lives.

Exercise 2-2: Looking at the SPACEGIS symptoms for yourself, which symptoms surfaced over the past twelve months? For each symptom, in what way are you now different than the normal you?

According to the American Psychological Association, when an individual suffers from a depressed mood and experiences four or more of the above symptoms for more than two weeks, the individual is depressed.

The PHQ-9 represents one of the most widely used depression screening instruments. The PHQ-9 refines the SPACEGIS assessment by quantifying the symptom severity. The individual simply checks off the frequency of each symptom over the past two weeks and totals the score (score the "Not at all" category as 0 in the Subtotals column). For example:

PHQ-9 Symptom Checklist (Kroenke, et al., 2001)				
Over the last 2 weeks, how often have you been bothered by the following problems?	Not at all	Several days	More than half the days	Nearly every day
a. Little interest or pleasure in doing things				√
b. Feeling down, depressed, or hopeless		√		
c. Trouble falling or staying asleep, or sleeping too much			√	
d. Feeling tired or having little energy				√
e. Poor appetite or overeating		√		
f. Feeling bad about yourself, or that you are a failure			√	
g. Trouble concentrating or things, such as reading				√
h. Moving or speaking slowly	√			
i. Thoughts that you would be better off dead		√		
Subtotals		3	4	9

TOTAL SCORE: 16

Typically, a total score under 5 is normal, the 5-9 range represents a minor depression, 10-14 represents a fairly mild to moderate range of major depression, 15-19 represents moderate to severe, and 20 and above represents a severe depression.

When left untreated, a mild depression (burnout)
almost always progresses into a major depression.

However, three conditions can stimulate the same symptoms as depression: 1) bereavement (within two months of loss), 2) some specific medical conditions, 3) or drugs. Thus, depression is ruled out when any of these three conditions exist. Ilardi (2009) notes that some medical conditions can induce depression symptoms including:

Hypothyroidism	Reproductive hormone
Anemia	dysregulation
Malnutrition	Stroke
Hepatitis	Dementia
Sleep Apnea	Heart Disease
Diabetes	Cancer

Some drugs that may induce depression symptoms include:

Beta-blockers	"The Pill" / HRT
Benzodiazepines such as	Fluroquinolone antibiotics such as
Ativan, Xanax, Klonopin	Cipro, Floxin
Alcohol	Anticonvulsants
Narcotics	

Always consult a physician when you first notice the symptoms of depression. The physician will need to rule out these conditions before prescribing any medication.

In North America, about 12%-14% of men and 22%-24% of women experience major depression at some time during their lifetimes. Of those who experience depression, about 80% will suffer from recurrent bouts over their career. For ministers, the rate seems about double the rate for secular individuals. For missionaries and pastors in countries outside North America, the rate seems higher yet. If Kroenke's data is correct, a downcast spirit and depression will negatively impact any mission or church agency's medical budget if not addressed with preventative care (i.e., preventative training in principles for resilience). More important than the medical expense, depression significantly reduces productivity of the average minister for at least two years when left untreated, causes conflict between coworkers, and negatively affects all team members including the entire church congregation.

Stephen Ilardi from the University of Kansas notes that when an individual experiences depression, the brain counters with a runaway stress response. That is, the hypothalamus affects the pituitary gland to release ACTH in the blood. This, in turn, affects the adrenal gland to release cortisol. Cortisol helps the individual to adapt to stress in the short-term. However, it acts harmfully over the long term. When abnormal levels of stress persist for more than 30 days, the brain reduces BDNF (a brain growth hormone), serotonin, and sleep becomes disturbed as the slow-wave sleep activity changes. Ilardi notes that chronic stress induces more than depression. It also induces brain changes (damage) in the cortex and hippocampus, deregulates the immune system, and increases inflammation.

Across the world, the risk of burnout and depression varies as a function of urbanization and industrialization—the more urban and industrialized societies that function like North America show higher incidences of depression and burnout. Stephen Ilardi notes that, "We were never designed for the modern sedentary, indoor, social isolated, fast-food-laden, frenzied, sleep-deprived way of life." Although the rural missionary compound still exists in some parts of the world, missionaries in many regions reside in multi-storied apartment complexes that stretch for mile after mile in highly industrialized cities. For most missionaries, urbanization and industrialization now characterize their third-world culture as much as the North American culture.

Remember Brian (mentioned at the beginning of this chapter)? Hearing a friend say, "Suck it up" failed to help him. Hearing someone else blame him for burnout and say, "Manage your stress better" also failed to help. He prayed every day for help. However, Brian is merely human, and so his body still responds to stress just as God designed it to respond. That is, when the stress persists for more than about 30 days, his brain reduces serotonin production, and he grows depressed.

Almost all of Brian's stressors, like the stressors common to most ministers and missionaries, remained totally outside of his control. Brian didn't ask for the unavoidable stress that comes with transitioning to a new church (326 units of stress). He didn't ask for a major auto accident (53 units of stress), vicarious stress brought by seven crises of members in his church (203 units of stress), conflict with another minister (23 units of stress), a chronic lack of security (29 units of stress), or the divorce of his child (44 units of stress). Brian simply responded to God's call, and the call led him into harm's way.

Initially, Brian found that God's call includes great joy. He also found that "the call" frequently includes great suffering, as described in the book of Job. When his friend said, "Suck it up," he implied that Brian failed to control his own feelings and that the solution remained totally within his own grasp. That is, his friend implied that if we feel bad, instead of turning to the Comforter, we can cope by simply telling ourselves to "Suck it up." This type of advice seems reminiscent of Job's friends who suggested that Job's plight resulted from his own sin.

Job's friends also told him to repent. Telling a minister or missionary to better manage his or her stress implies that he or she needs to repent of a stressful lifestyle. Similarly, telling a minister to pray harder seems similar to telling him or her that they have failed to pray hard enough. Reflect for a moment: How would Job feel if you told him to, "Suck it up," or "Manage your stress better" or "Pray harder"? How would these statements help Job?

Job's friends failed to realize that he lived in the middle of a struggle between God and Satan, and Job retained no control over God or

Satan. Likewise, most ministers retain little or no control over their environment. Their stress often results from the sinful ways of a godless society and a fallen world. Like Job, ministers and missionaries sometimes suffer from the invading Sabeans (see Job 1:15) or Chaldeans (see Job 1:17) who steal and kill.

A healthy environment excludes assault, robbery, murder, kidnapping, man-made crises, and natural disasters. Sometimes we acculturate ourselves to a godless environment so thoroughly that we begin to see these sins as normal and our response as abnormal. However, Job's feelings and responses remained normal. His environment was abnormal. Likewise, the minister's response of burnout is usually normal, and his or her environment remains sinful and therefore abnormal.

In contrast to Job's (and Brian's) friends, Jesus says, "Blessed are the poor in spirit, for theirs is the kingdom of heaven (Matthew 5:3)." "Come to me, all you who are weary and burdened, and I will give you rest. Take my yoke upon you and learn from me, for I am gentle and humble in heart, and you will find rest for your souls" (Matthew 11:28-30, NIV). Jesus never claims to prevent us from feeling "weary and burdened." He simply invites the weary and burdened to find rest in Him. Like Job, ministers suffer from the Chaldeans, and like Job, ministers are transformed by revelation.

Like Job, we will all stand, silenced, acknowledging our ignorance. We tremble at offering counsel in fear that God might find as much fault with us as He found with Job's friends. However, we can sit with those in need. We can offer a cup of water (physical, emotional, and spiritual help). And we pass along transforming revelation as inspired by the Spirit.

Post traumatic stress disorder (PTSD)

Post-Traumatic Stress Disorder (PTSD) results from an incident that involves actual or threatened death or serious injury. A minister may never experience PTSD, but he or she will almost certainly see it numerous times within the church membership and greater community. As the minister tries to help those with PTSD, the minister will suffer the normal stress from those actions. PTSD results from experiences such as:

- Severe auto accidents—now tied with armed robbery as the leading cause of death for missionaries worldwide
- Armed robbery—especially common throughout Latin America, Africa, Eurasia, and Eastern Europe
- Physical assault
- Rape
- Car-jacking—especially common throughout Latin America, Africa, Eurasia, and Eastern Europe
- Kidnapping—common in Latin America and Africa
- Civil war and insurrection—almost a norm in much of Africa
- Natural disasters
- Expulsion—always a problem in sensitive countries, but now increasingly common even in Western Europe
- Witnessing any of the above

When any of these crises threaten death or physical injury, or when an individual witnesses death or physical injury, PTSD grows into a significant possibility. Many missionaries assume that they remain resistant to PTSD as long as they avoid the above experiences. However, they usually overlook that witnessing any of the above incidents makes them susceptible and remains the most overlooked and most frequent source of PTSD for missionaries. Witnessing these events in your congregation can also lead to PTSD.

Witnessing or experiencing any single above event, by itself, can easily induce Post Traumatic Stress Disorder (PTSD). The Diagnostic Statistic Manual IV indicates that PTSD results whenever a victim experiences the following:

1. Actual or threatened death or serious injury, or witnessing death or physical injury
2. The individual's response includes intense fear, helplessness, or horror
3. And the individual experiences the following symptoms for at least one month:
    a. Persistent re-experiencing of the traumatic event
    b. Persistent avoidance of stimuli associated with the traumatic event
    c. And persistent symptoms of arousal such as sleeplessness, anxiety, hyper-vigilance, or increased levels of energy
4. And the symptoms cause distress in work and social functioning.

For condition 3.a. above, the event can be re-experienced through intrusive memories, recurrent nightmares, or flashbacks. Flashbacks occur when the individual relives and behaves as though the event is happening all over again.

For condition 3.b. above, the individual feels intense distress when exposed to cues that symbolize the event. For instance, a firecracker is mistaken for a gunshot. So the individual usually tries to avoid thoughts, feelings, or conversations about the event. The individual especially tries to avoid places or people associated with the event.

PTSD is associated with increased rates for depression, panic disorder, Generalized Anxiety Disorder, Obsessive-Compulsive Disorder, Agoraphobia (fear of going outside), Social Phobia and Bipolar Disorder. The victim often feels intense guilt over surviving the traumatic event.

How susceptible am I to PTSD?

The lifetime incidence of PTSD in the U.S.A. is 8%. Thus, almost every minister will find numerous PTSD victims within their community. For missionaries, however, the incidence remains 4-10 times higher, depending on the country in which they live. Twenty percent of women develop PTSD after a traumatic event. Thirty percent of Vietnam combat veterans and 50% of POWs develop PTSD. Other than witnessing any of the above incidents, the most common source of missionary PTSD remains a serious auto accident or armed robbery. Regardless the incident, repeated exposure to any the above incidents increases the vulnerability to PTSD from a later incident. So by the third incident, the individual grows four times more likely to suffer from PTSD. And so in some countries, almost all missionaries and many other ministers eventually experience PTSD, usually after repeated exposure to multiple incidents. Their colleagues sometimes wonder why a seemingly relatively minor incident suddenly results in major problems, when all along, the minister gradually grew increasingly vulnerable to PTSD. The analogy of "the final straw that broke the camel's back" applies to ministers more than many realize. However, with PTSD each successive straw (incident) weighs twice as much as the former.

PTSD often begins immediately after exposure to an incident, but sometimes emerges as much as 30 years later. A Vietnam veteran friend of mine suddenly experienced disabling symptoms over 30 years after leaving Vietnam. The Harvard Mental Health Letter describes it:

> Victims are often edgy, irritable, easily startled, and constantly on guard: the Vietnam veteran always sits with his back to the wall; the rape victim watches for potential rapists everywhere. Victims sleep poorly; they are agitated and find it difficult to concentrate. This group of symptoms is often described as hyperalertness or hyperarousal.

When not experiencing the above symptoms, the victims often experience numbing. Numbing includes a desire to avoid feelings, thoughts and situations that remind them of the incident, or a loss of emotions altogether. The victim notes that they cease to feel that anything matters. They feel cut-off from other individuals. Their feelings seem unnatural because they feel numbed to almost everything around them.

While adults often experience nightmares about the incident, children experience more generalized nightmares about monsters and demons. Instead of reliving an event, they re-enact it in their day-dreams and play. They tend to complain of all sorts of aches and pains, talk like a baby again, and some resort to wetting their pants like a toddler.

How does PTSD affect the children of ministers?

Childhood PTSD seems to induce borderline personality disorder in the adult years. The symptoms of a borderline personality include instability in mood, thinking, behavior, interpersonal relationships, and self-image. Borderline personalities are difficult to live with. Their friends and relatives note that the borderline personality presents unreasonable demands, provocative behavior, tantrums, hypochondriacal complaints, and suicide threats. These individuals seem chronically disagreeable, short tempered, and easily offended. Friends often feel dismayed that these individuals who seem so insensitive toward others can respond with hypersensitivity to anything that affects themselves. These individuals almost always experience multiple divorces and seem particularly susceptible to alcohol abuse. Without doubt, many adult children of ministers and missionaries suffer as lifelong borderline personality as adults due to their untreated childhood PTSD.

What should I do about PTSD?

First, realize that much hope exists. Two years after their release, I (Nathan) debriefed a group of POWs. All suffered from PTSD as a result of intense torture by the Taliban. After the intervention, all reported an immediate cessation of nightmares. Twelve recovered fully from other symptoms within a year and all recovered fully within two years. Similarly, a missionary contacted us who suffered from PTSD including daily nightmares for nearly two years after an incident of physical assault and battery. After the intervention, she reported an immediate total cessation of nightmares, and within one year she reported a total cessation of all other symptoms.

Thus, intervention works. Please reject the notion that you simply need to work through it. Without intervention, PTSD almost always destroys work effectiveness and all relationships with family and coworkers. In as little as two or three hours, someone can lead the victim through a process that usually helps considerably. Sometimes the process requires repeated interventions, but the process works. Almost no one needs to suffer from chronic PTSD.

Second, note that PTSD occurs as a *normal* result of an *abnormal* event. Since the victim feels abnormal, they and their colleagues often assume that the victim is abnormal. They are wrong. The victim's bodily response (with PTSD) remains a *normal* response to an *abnormal* event. When you see a missionary or other minister who seems to act abnormally, instead of blaming them, ask yourself, "What event has this person experienced that stimulates them to act this way?" Almost always, their behavior follows as a *normal* result of a very *abnormal* event. We invite you to avoid blaming yourself and fellow ministers for something that seems almost inevitable in many countries. Let's *normalize* PTSD. Blame the abnormal event, not the victim.

PTSD remains a normal experience for many ministers and even some of their parishioners and members of their community. However, great hope remains with intervention.

Hope remains

In *A Psalm in Your Heart* (125) Dr. George Wood addresses the appropriate response to stressful events like those that affected King David (see Psalm 31). He relates a narrative between Wayne Kraiss and an elderly woman about her bedridden childhood.

> When I was a little girl in Germany, one day I asked my mother what it means that "all things work together for good." My mother was baking a cake and, without directly answering my question, she handed me a

spoonful of baking soda. It tasted awful. Finally, I asked her what she was doing and she responded that she was answering my question. "Amelia, my mother said, "I don't want you to ever forget that all things taken by themselves are not always pleasant. But when they are mixed together and fired in the oven, you love the results.""

Dr. George Wood ends with the following prayer:

Lord, I don't like the taste of a bitter experience but I trust you with the outcome. Forgive me for thinking the ingredient was your final product. With David, I confess, "How great is your goodness which you have stored up for [me]."

What if I suffer from burnout, depression, or PTSD?

If like Brian, you suffer from clinical depression or PTSD, don't despair. For many ministers, these normal vocational hazards result from responding to a sinful society and a fallen world.

We hope to enhance your learning experience with video clips that illustrate the concepts in this book. When instructed to do so, please access a YouTube playlist available at:

http://www.youtube.com/playlist?list=PL72D988EF1CB77905

If you presently suffer from depression, please access the playlist and view the video clip, "Treating Depression (Part 3 of 4) HealthiNation."

This book *never* offers therapy. This book provides prevention and resilience skills. If you presently suffer from depression or PTSD, please see a psychologist or physician right away. Both depression and PTSD remain highly treatable.

CHAPTER 3

Pay a Little Now, or Pay a Lot Later

In the early 1960s, an American astronaut asked the startling question, "How would you feel if you knew that the lowest priced contractor built the rocket on which you ride?" His question startled NASA to pay a little more attention to the initial planning and design phase to avoid a high-cost catastrophe, later. Likewise, most of us acknowledge the need to pay a little for oil changes on our car to avoid a high cost engine failure. And, the wise minister, missionary, and chaplain will also pay a little time now to prepare for an inevitable crisis, later.

My family arrived in Japan in 1959, and within a few months, my parents noted that I would likely fall victim to at least four types of crises:

- Robbery
- Earthquakes
- Separation from family
- Molestation

Robbery

In 1959, my parents explained that burglary would likely occur sometime during our first term. They never postulated what to do *if* it occurred. Their instruction always focused on what to do *when* it occurred. As a child, I accepted the inevitability, and they helped me plan and practice what to do when it occurred. They explained that burglary would likely occur while I slept and that my actions should be quite different if I awakened to find the burglar outside the house (trying to gain entrance) than if I awakened to find the burglar already inside. After explaining the appropriate and inappropriate behaviors for each circumstance, they led me to practice each appropriate response. Within a year, I awakened one night to find someone trying to open the window above my head. My parents' instruction flooded my mind, and I quickly jumped out of bed and sprang into well-practiced action. Within seconds, I frightened away the burglar and my father was running outside to ensure his speedy departure! My parents' investment in one hour of pre-planning and practice paid great dividends.

Earthquakes

Japan sits atop a major fault line in the earth's crust, so earthquakes seem normal. Within a few months of arriving in Japan, my parents explained what to do during an earthquake. They showed me the safest part of the house to which I should run and demonstrated how to react upon arrival there. Within six months, we experienced a big one. However, I knew exactly what to do. I remembered their instruction because they helped me to practice it; and therefore, I felt safe. Over the next nine years, I experienced innumerable earthquakes. I felt reassured and safe because I knew exactly what to do. Once again, my parents' investment in one hour of pre-planning and practice paid great dividends.

Separation from family

After riding a Japanese commuter train during a 1959 rush hour, my parents recognized the high probability that the crowd could easily separate our family while boarding a train. During rush hour, a herd of people getting off the train would push away individuals standing near the doors. Eventually, professional pushers would press those remaining on the platform back onto the train. Within seconds, the doors would suddenly close and the train would start down the track to the next station. My parents foresaw that someone in our family might get left behind, so they devised a plan for what to do when (not if) that happened. And within three months, I calmly waived to my parents on the platform while the train (with me onboard) pulled out of the station. I felt calm because I knew exactly what to do. We had trained for it, rehearsed it, and I knew that our plan would work. For some reason that I never understood until I became a parent, my mother didn't look very calm as I departed on that train, alone. However, each of us followed our well-honed plan and within 15 minutes I reunited with some extremely happy parents. Their pre-planning paid great dividends.

Molestation

Upon arriving in Japan, my parents noted the lack of Christian values. They asked a reasonable question, *"If molestation happens to those in the States, how much more will it happen to those who serve in a nearly godless culture?"* So, they explained to me what molestation would look like, and what to do when (not if) it happened. As a ten year old MK, I couldn't imagine that anyone would try what they described. However, within two years, a man attempted to molest me. Because of my father's explicit description, I immediately recognized what was happening, and I ran the other way. I was saved not by my innocence but by my father's foresight and pre-planning.

Of the many couples who relate their story to me about their child's molestation, one couple's story stays in the front of my mind. They were the first who told me about the pre-crisis instruction they gave to their small son. At a very young age, they prepared him with knowledge of what molestation would look like, and encouraged him to tell them if anyone tried to touch him inappropriately. Therefore, he quickly let them know when this happened. Even while observing the pain of their story, I experienced relief. Their wisdom had saved their child from years of unspeakable horror and guilt. They cried because of what *could* have happened, not because of what *had* happened.

Over half of North Americans state that they accept Christian values, and about one third claim to be "born again." Yet, about sixteen percent of adolescent males experience molestation, and about fifty percent of adolescent females experience molestation. If the molestation rate seems high in the North American Christian culture, then what is a realistic expectation of molestation for MKs raised in a non-Christian culture? If you work as a minister, expect that others will try to molest your children. Even Christians sometimes retain addictions to ungodly lifestyles that became habits before conversion. And since you work and live among ungodly people, expect ungodly people to act ungodly.

As an MK in Japan, I lived in one of the safest countries in the world. Yet, by the age of eighteen, I experienced each of the above four crises. Additionally, I encountered three other crises—an incident of assault and battery, my most beloved high school teacher was murdered by anti-American protestors, and then the perpetrators of the murder returned to kill me. If I experienced these crises living in one of the safest countries in the world, what is the probability that you and your children will avoid crises in the culture to which you live?

Consider the probability of crisis in your family based on the country and culture to which God calls you.

Exercise 3-1: List the traumas and crises that characterize your culture and region.

Auto accident—

Robbery—

Assault—

Molestation—

Typhoon or hurricane—

Tornado—

Flood—

Earthquake—

Insurrection—

Civil war—

Kidnapping—

Hijacking—

Other—

Chronic Environments:

Gender discrimination—

Ethnic discrimination—

Emotional rejection—

Discrimination against or rejection of Christians—

Other—

Exercise 3-2: What is your step-by-step plan to avoid and counteract each crisis?

Exercise 3-3: We invite you to pay a little now to avoid paying a lot later. Please discuss your potential crises and coordinate your plans with your leadership.

CHAPTER 4

A Model to Help Those in Crisis

"….happens." At least that is what I (Nathan) commonly heard when I worked for the Air Force. A much as I detested that type of language, I knew exactly what the speaker meant. That is, stuff happens. Since the fall of humankind, crises have continued to this day. And in addition to the normal human expectation of death and taxes, we can be sure that a crisis will visit each of us and each person in our community sometime in the future. If nothing bad is happening to you right now, just wait—"Stuff happens."

Research indicates that when an individual experiences a crisis, within the next two years he or she will almost always also experience a crisis of faith. Christians will experience a crisis of their faith, and Muslims, Buddhists, Hindus, animists, and every other person will also experience a crisis of faith regardless their belief system. This almost universal crisis of faith presents an excellent opportunity for local pastors and missionaries to fill that spiritual void with God's love and message.

When local pastors equip themselves to respond appropriately to a crisis, the gospel message almost always receives a welcome response even from the most spiritually resistant victim. Thankfully, crisis care consumes only a small part of pastoral care ministry.

Crisis care offers an unsurpassed opportunity
to teach and rebuild resilience skills,
especially relating to spiritual resilience.

When helping other Christians in crisis, I warn them that their upcoming crisis of faith results as a normal outcome of their recent crisis. When (not if) the desire to quit finally arrives, don't quit—accept the feeling as a normal but transient feeling that will pass usually within the next year. Those who quit as a result of a crisis almost always regret their emotion-based decision.

When ministering to those in crisis, we recommend a seven step model to help them rebuild their resilience and find a new normal:

1. Set the ground rules
2. Stimulate verbalization of the crisis events
3. Validate the victim's thoughts and emotions
4. Assess the common emotional symptoms (see Chapter 2)
5. Teach skills for physical resilience (see Chapters 5-8)
6. Teach skills for emotional resilience (see Chapters 9-14)
7. Teach skills for spiritual resilience (see Chapters 15-18)

Step 1—Set the ground rules

When helping others in crisis, start by introducing yourself and asking the other individuals to introduce themselves. Then, establish the ground rules for your time together:

- First, address the issue of confidentiality. Let them know that other than legal requirements to report child molestation, or a plan to harm themselves or someone else, you pledge to maintain confidentiality about everything in the session.

- Meet in a place with no distractions, and ask them to turn off all pagers and cell phones.

- If you meet with several individuals as a group, make sure that everyone in the group experienced the same incident. Your goal remains to help the victims. Therefore, avoid including anyone who failed to witness the incident, in person; you cannot guarantee their confidentiality or understanding.

- Commit to spend two or three sessions with the group or with each individual, and set up the time and date for the next follow-on session.

- Keep each session less than 2.5 hours, ending no later than 8:00 p.m. Longer sessions abuse both you and the victim.

- If you meet with several victims in the same session, limit the group size to no more than three or four individuals. Larger groups require too much time, and exhaust the participants and the minister.

- Observe normal guidelines that restrict cross-gender counseling and ministry.

Exercise 4-1: Practice this first step until you can set the ground rules in less than ten minutes.

Step 2—Stimulate verbalization of the crisis events

Healing starts as we verbally process our crisis. Verbalization provides an extremely important intervention—it activates a different part of the brain than used for non-verbal tasks. Ask each individual to describe the incident from their own perspective. Specifically ask them to describe their role and the top-level facts that occurred sequentially during the incident, such as who did what and when. When we ask victims to narrate only the facts and events, they usually feel secure in the knowledge that they can avoid digging into their raw hurts and emotions. Start by asking them to relate only the top-level facts and sequence of events.

For instance, some friends and I (Nathan) experienced an incident as we flew a small plane over the Ozark Mountains. If another minister agreed to "debrief" me about the incident, he might ask me to relate the facts and sequence of events. I would respond by saying:

> While flying at about 12,000 feet, our airplane engine suddenly quit. Our pilot kept trying to restart the engine, but it never restarted. Finally, he called out a "mayday" with our position and started to glide in a slow circle looking for a place to land. We saw nothing but forest and mountains. As we gradually descended, we noticed two open fields at 90° to each other. We headed for the larger field, but as we got lower, we noticed a herd of cows in it. So we turned toward the smaller field. As we turned toward it, we suddenly noticed high-tension power lines between us and the field. We had descended so much that the top power line was already at an altitude higher than our airplane.

Notice that the above narration avoids any mention of thoughts or emotions even though I felt plenty of emotions. It focuses merely on the facts and sequence of events that occurred— who did what, when.

While listening to the narration, avoid assigning blame or judgment. During this step, some individuals tend to step ahead by describing their thoughts and feelings. If that happens, let them include that broader description, too. After all, you will ask them to relate their thoughts and emotions in the next step, anyway.

PTSD victims often want to avoid this step—they especially dislike describing their crisis to a group. If anyone feels reluctant to participate in a group, set up a separate session just for them.

When a victim experiences multiple crises such as happens in war or by torture, lead them to describe each crisis separately. For instance, I (Nathan) debriefed a group of POWs who experienced daily torture. Instead of asking the victims to describe their entire time of imprisonment, I asked them to narrate their daily events, one day at a time until they described their entire imprisonment. By describing each day separately, they could delve deeper into each crisis without confusing each event with another.

Exercise 4-2: Practice this second step until you can complete it in ten or fifteen minutes when debriefing an individual.

Step 3—Validate the victim's thoughts and emotions

In order to validate their thoughts and feelings, first ask each individual to describe the thoughts and feelings they experienced during each part of the incident. Start by recalling their first recollection of the incident, and ask about their thoughts and feelings at that time. Then proceed slowly through their entire incident description, asking them to recall their thoughts and feeling during each stage of the incident. Some individuals recall their feelings quickly, and some find difficulty with the process. For those who find difficult with identifying their feelings, feel free to prompt them by asking about their surface level feelings and their deep level feelings.

Surface feelings such as:

Unhappy	Angry
Envious	Shame
Fearful	Sadness
Nervous/Stressed out	Hurt

Deep feelings such as:

Out of Control	Unrecognized	Unvalued

Unloved   Unappreciated   Unaccepted
Honesty is questioned
Continuing with the same airplane incident used above, I would describe my thoughts and feelings as follows:

> When the engine of the small plane quit, I looked down and saw nothing but mountains and trees. My first thought was, "I am going to die today." As I reflected on my impending death, I felt surprised at my lack of fear. I distinctly remember thinking, "I will soon be 'at home' with God, and therefore have nothing to fear." I also felt reassured that I had previously bought a life insurance policy that would financially support my family.

An individual debriefing me would probably paraphrase what I thought about my impending death. Then, he or she would probably proceed to ask me about my thoughts and feelings during each part of the remainder of the story, including how I felt when I first realized that I survived. I will conclude this story in a later chapter of this book.

During this step, many victims show tears. However, some don't. Avoid trying to prompt tears. The minister's role remains to validate the victim's thoughts and feelings, not the minister's reaction to their experience. This requires you to adopt a non-judgmental listening attitude that invites them to tell their story, including the facts, thoughts, and emotions. As they verbalize their story in a safe and non-judgmental environment, healing begins.

Those with PTSD may need to retell their story numerous times over a many months, and sometimes over many years. As a general rule, the sooner victim tells their story, the better. The longer they wait, the more times they will probably need to retell their story. For instance, a missionary victim of assault and battery eliminated his PTSD symptoms within only a few sessions. However, he started telling his story within a week after the assault. In contrast, a war veteran who waited 30 years still needs to retell his story because of recurrent symptoms.

Exercise 4-3: Practice this third step until you can complete it in less than thirty minutes when debriefing a single individual.

Step 4—Assess the common emotional symptoms

Please reference chapter 2 for a list of the SPACEGIS symptoms, the PHQ-9 symptoms, and the PTSD symptoms. Memorize these lists. I (Nathan) start the assessment by asking about the SPACEGIS symptoms. I only proceed to the PHQ-9 checklist when the SPACEGIS symptoms indicate a depression or anxiety problem. In every case, stress that symptoms and feelings occur as a *normal* result of the incident. The incident remains abnormal, but feelings are normal. If the symptoms indicate a possibility of depression, anxiety disorder, or PTSD, make referrals to a psychologist or a physician if one exists in your country. Similar symptoms result from many medical causes, and a physician needs to rule out those causes before prescribing any medication.

If the victim seems to suffer from an emotional problem, let him or her know that they *SEEM* to suffer from some symptoms. However, avoid scaring the victim with a diagnosis. Since some medications and illnesses can mimic any disorder, let a physician or licensed psychologist make the diagnosis. Limit your role to referral and teaching resilience skills to help the victim.

Exercise 4-4: Practice this fourth step until you can complete the SPACEGIS assessment in less than fifteen minutes.

Step 5—Teach skills for physical resilience

The three teaching steps serve as the most important steps in the process. Never shortchange these steps. Teach the skills for physical resilience described in Chapters 5-8. Ask individuals to commit to implement each skill. Coach them in developing an implementation plan for each skill. Help them identify potential accountability partners. This step usually takes about an hour.

Step 6—Teach skills for emotional resilience

While an incident often represents the external event that causes a transition, transition represents the emotional upheaval within an individual. A transition is a phase that results when incidents or events change the individual's roles, relationships, routines, and expectations. Often, individuals worry about the external change while their internal transition remains unnoticed. However, every stressor listed on the Holmes and Rahe (1967) table in Chapter 2 functions as a change that induces transition along with an emotional response. Transitions, even when functioning as a positive transition, produce stress. So transition remains a normal and unavoidable fact of every minister's life. And each minister gets to help others during their transitions.

> Worry about the transition
> even more than the change.

Ministers often spend more time trying to control the change than the transition. For instance, a minister who faces imminent dismissal from a church might fight the change by trying to form alliances with key church members while encouraging disgruntled church members to move to another church. Meanwhile, the conflict alters the pastor's roles, relationships, and expectations within that same church. The transition in roles, relationships, and expectations almost always produces emotional turmoil and consumes a large amount of energy. And the transition often requires the minister to reframe his or her core identity and learn new skills. While the external change often remains uncontrollable, the skills for emotional resilience (see Chapters 9 through 14) make the transition almost totally controllable.

In step 6, teach the skills for emotional resilience discussed in

Chapters 9 through 14. Especially describe the importance of socialization (Chapter 9) and reversing rumination (Chapter 10). Introduce the individual to goal setting as described in Chapters 12 and 13, but assign the goal setting as homework. Excluding Chapters 12 and 13, an overview of step six usually takes about thirty minutes. Address the skills in Chapters 12 and 13 on a following visit.

Creative output is influenced more by experience in a field (career age) than by chronological age (Cohen 2001, 108). Thus, regardless the crisis event, the individual has more creative aptitude to offer the Kingdom of God after their transition than at any previous time of life.

Step 7—Teach skills for spiritual resilience

Teach the skills for spiritual resilience in Chapters 15-19, especially focusing on the importance of thankfulness (Chapter 17) and hope (Chapter 18). Try to start on day one of the thankfulness exercise. Finish with the hope exercise at the end of the hope chapter. It will help them reframe a crisis into a positive experience. Note that some individuals feel unable to complete the hope exercise when first introduced to it. If they feel uncomfortable with the questions in the hope exercise, leave the exercise for a follow-on session. Although this step can last as briefly as five minutes, it usually gets postponed into a follow-on session in which the minister can spend more time. After all, for a minister this final step remains the most important.

Immediately after a crisis, very few victims feel able to remember and implement all the resilience skills discussed in this book. A crisis will commonly impede their ability to focus and concentrate. Therefore, the victim may feel unable to address the hope exercise for many months. When possible, leave a copy of this book as a resource guide for building physical, emotional, and spiritual resilience. Schedule follow-up sessions to coach individuals in implementing the resilience skills.

Please avoid trying to use the suggested crisis response model for every type of pastoral care ministry. The model applies only to those in crisis. Many individuals seek help and counsel for reasons other than a crisis. However, helping others with physical, emotional, and spiritual resilience forms the backbone of a major part of pastoral care ministry.

PART II:

How to Build

Physical Resilience

Physical resilience—what is it?

Burnout and depression result primarily from a lack of serotonin, norepinephrine and a few other important chemicals in the brain. Part II, How to Build Physical Resilience, presents research-proven lifestyles that physically stimulate the brain to produce serotonin and other important brain chemicals. These chemicals provide a physical margin of resilience against burnout and depression. However, stress degrades the brain's ability to produce these chemicals. And as chronic stress decreases the ability of the brain to produce these chemicals, the brain slows to the point at which an individual feels clinically depressed.

Unfortunately, the "blood-brain-barrier" prevents any pill or supplement from providing serotonin to the brain. These "brain" chemicals may keep the brain working at optimum performance levels, but they are produced only within the brain. Fortunately, research by Stephen Ilardi (2009) and others show that specific lifestyle behaviors stimulate the brain to physically increase its production of serotonin and other brain chemicals.

Repeatedly in the book of Psalms, King David describes emotions indicating that he probably experienced one or more episodes of major depression. However, King David rebounded, arguably, for two reasons:

1. He consistently put his trust in God.
2. His culture required him to adopt a lifestyle that automatically promoted physical resilience.

Many modern Christians neglect the lifestyles that promoted King David's physical resilience. Due to this neglect, the depression rate in North America has soared 1000% over the past 50 years (U.S. Department of Health and Human Services, 1999). Even more than their secular counterparts, twenty-first century ministers tend to neglect their physical resilience. This neglect leaves them much more susceptible to burnout and depression than their counterparts from earlier centuries.

Physical Resilience Assessment

Please score the below items as a 0, 1, 3, or 5, indicating the frequency with which you accomplish the activity during each week.

0 = I almost never accomplish this activity.

1 = I accomplish this activity about one time per week

3 = I accomplish this activity about three times per week.

5 = I accomplish this activity about five times per week.

Assessment A

	I exercise aerobically for at least 30 minutes.
	I eat broiled fish, baked fish, or take an Omega-3 supplement.
	I eat green leafy vegetables.
	I sleep soundly for seven or more hours at night.
	I receive about 30 minutes of continuous, direct sunlight.

_____ Total A Score

Assessment B

	I eat fried food.
	I eat food made from flour.
	I eat meat raised from grain.

_____ Total B Score

The following lifestyles, discussed in the next four chapters, build a physical margin of resilience by stimulating the brain to produce serotonin and a few critically important brain chemicals:

1. Aerobic Exercise
2. Omega-3 rich food

3. Deep sleep
4. Daily sunlight

How to score your physical resilience self-assessment

Total the scores for your assessment A items to find your Total A Score. Total the scores for your assessment B items to find your Total B Score. Subtract your Total B Score from your Total A Score to obtain your Physical Resilience Score.

Total A Score - Total B Score = Physical Resilience Score

If your physical resilience score is:

0-9 = Your physical resilience is seriously degraded. You are highly susceptible to burnout. You can benefit significantly from this section.

10-17 = Your physical resilience is marginal. Only one or two crises may stimulate burnout. You can benefit from some chapters in this section.

18-25 = Your physical resilience is fairly good at this time. Please read the chapters in this section to better understand how to keep yourself physically resilient.

For additional information on physical resilience, we highly recommend *The Depression Cure*, by Stephen Ilardi (2009). To see an overview of this book and factors that affect physical resilience, please access the YouTube playlist referenced on page 31, and view the following video clips on the playlist:

- Interview with Dr. Steven Ilardi Part 1
- Interview with Dr. Steven Ilardi Part 2
- The Serotonin System and Depression (4 of 11)
- The Serotonin System and Depression (5 of 11)
- How SSRIs and MAO Inhibitors Work

CHAPTER 5

Physical Resilience by Deep Sleep

What makes sleep so important?

Slow-wave sleep (deep sleep) stimulates the production of serotonin and other depression-fighting chemicals in the brain. The lack of these chemicals causes depression. Chemically, depression represents nothing more than the lack of serotonin and other chemicals that are produced by the brain during sleep. Thus, sleep builds crucial chemicals that prevent a downcast spirit and depression. God designed the human body to sleep—and important illness preventative brain functions occur while we sleep.

For ministers in stressful assignments, the lack of sleep eventually catches up with them. Depression results and kills their motivation to work for about two years. Sadly, I see dozens of ministers every year who experience burnout, almost always induced by unforeseen crises. Without enough margin that results from sleep, they unwittingly grow susceptible to burnout. Their resilience margin shrinks in a slow and insidious process that goes unnoticed. They usually function well for several years as their margin gradually dwindles. Then suddenly, an unforeseen crisis or two puts them beyond their ability to cope.

Stephen Ilardi (2009, 35-36) explains the process as follows: When laboratory rats are experimentally deprived of slow-wave sleep for several days at a time, their brains start to malfunction and they become seriously ill. Humans react in much the same way. After just a few nights of slow-wave sleep deprivation, most people report intense, aching fatigue. After a few more days, they begin to feel physically ill. They also start moving and speaking more slowly. Many people even complain of a sensation of physical pain (even though they can't quite tell where it's coming from). In this sleep-altered state, mood turns despondent, social interest disappears, thoughts turn negative, appetite becomes erratic, and concentration wanes. In other words, with the disappearance of slow-wave sleep, the core symptoms of depression quickly emerge.

Thus, inadequate sleep stimulates a downcast spirit and depression. When adults consistently shortchange their sleep by a couple of hours per night, they grow increasingly susceptibility to depression. Their margin gradually wanes over a period of months and even years. After their margin dwindles completely, most bouts with depression start with several weeks of chronic sleeplessness. And, most depressed individuals often find themselves awake in the middle of the night—they simply cannot remain asleep. Their normal slow-wave sleep pattern gets totally disrupted.

What sleep behaviors characterized Adam and Eve's lifestyle?

At what time of the evening did Adam and Eve go to bed? Without the advent of electric lights they probably went to sleep shortly after sundown. Possibly, they lit a campfire for an hour or two, but after a hard day of tending a rather large garden, they probably fell asleep as soon as the fire subsided and maybe even before that.

At what time of the morning did Adam and Eve awake? We don't really know when they awoke, but without alarm clocks to awake them, they probably stayed asleep until the sun came up.

Thus, how many hours did Adam and Eve sleep? Again, we can't say exactly where they lived or how many hours they slept each night. However, if they lived near the present Tigris and Euphrates rivers, sunrise and sunset were probably around 6 a.m. and 6 p.m. Thus, after allowing them to sit around a campfire for an hour or two in the evening, they probably slept at least eight hours per night, maybe even as much as ten hours per night.

Interestingly, individuals in most of the primitive cultures of the world still sleep eight to ten hours per day.

When we choose a different lifestyle than the one designed by God, we may suffer some consequences.

How does Adam and Eve's probable sleep pattern compare to yours?

When I ask this question of ministers, I usually see a lot of smiles and hear a lot of chuckles. In two recent seminars (of about 130 participants each), only 5-6 raised their hands when I asked how many sleep at least 8 hours per night. Usually, a hard-core few appear proud of their "work ethic." If they behaved conscientiously, however, they would build up a margin against burnout supported through sufficient sleep.

Just like Adam and Eve, we are made in God's image. So we share similar strengths and weaknesses to Adam and Eve. God designed an environment that almost forced Adam and Eve to sleep eight or more hours each night. Today, technology enables humankind to literally "burn the candle at both ends," working late into the night and rising to start work well before dawn. Because of electricity, we can choose a significantly different model of rest than the one He provided. While electricity can serve humankind in a wonderful way, we can use it to abuse ourselves.

How much sleep do I need?

Most individuals need at least eight hours of sleep per night. During this time, the brain replaces a large amount of the serotonin that gets consumed during the day. Usually, the replacement process takes at least eight hours. If you lead a highly stressful life, you may need more. Thus, without at least eight hours of sleep, your margin against burnout and depression gradually dwindles away. Some ministers get by with less than eight hours of sleep, but even one extra crisis or an unexpected stressor leaves them with an insufficient margin against burnout and depression. Rather than asking, "How much sleep do I need," we invite you to ask, "Given the level of stress in my lifestyle and the potential for crises in my work and country, how much margin do I want against burnout?"

Is your "call" important enough to prevent burnout?

The American Sleep Foundation reports that the average North American secular individual obtains 6.7 hours of sleep each night. I find that many ministers sleep less than the average secular individual. In addition to seminar participants, numerous pastors and missionaries within my fellowship report that they get only five to six hours of sleep.

Frequently, when I ask ministers to get eight hours of sleep, they respond that they simply can't stay asleep that long. They suffer from insomnia. Their insomnia often stems from unhealthy sleep habits that they carefully honed over many decades. I advise them to start by replacing bad habits with the following behaviors, recommended by Ilardi and many others.

Get a physical checkup. Sleep apnea, hyperthyroidism, chronic pain and several other physical problems inhibit sleep. If you find difficulty with insomnia, get a physical checkup to determine if a medical problem prevents sleep. If a medical problem inhibits your sleep, address it immediately. Whatever threatens your sleep, threatens your ministry.

Avoid violent movies and TV shows in the evening. Violence stimulates the brain for about two hours and causes insomnia. Avoid anything that includes violence (including news shows that depict violence) at least two hours before bedtime.

Turn off the TV at least 30 minutes before bedtime. When we watch TV, the story continues to stimulate our brain even after we turn it off. At least 30 minutes before bedtime, turn off the TV and let your brain focus on getting ready for bed.

Retain your bedroom only for sleep. This rule gradually trains your body to expect sleep whenever you get into bed. Thus avoid reading, sowing, eating, and other activities in bed. Sex is the only exception to this rule. Sex releases serotonin which aids sleep.

Avoid caffeine and alcohol at least 8 hours before bedtime. The half-life of caffeine is approximately 4.9 hours. In women taking oral contraceptives this is increased to five to ten hours. And in pregnant women the half-life is roughly nine to eleven hours. Consuming two or more cups of coffee increases the half-life even longer. Common caffeine levels (shown by Wikipedia) are:

Product	Mg of Caffeine per serving
Drip coffee	115–175
Percolated coffee	80–135
Coffee, espresso	100
Coffee, decaffeinated	5-15
Black tea	50

Green tea	30
Coca-Cola Classic	34
Dark chocolate (45% cacao content)	31

The body can metabolize one ounce of alcohol per hour. So many individuals assume that a drink or two in the evening affects their sleep minimally. However, alcohol also dehydrates the body. So these same individuals often wake up thirsty in the middle of the night. If you drink alcohol, try to avoid it within three hours of bedtime. If you drink within four hours of bedtime, rehydrate your body with extra water.

Avoid sleep anywhere other than your bed. Train your body to recognize that sleep goes with your bed, but not elsewhere.

After lying awake for 15-20 minutes, leave the bedroom and find something relaxing to do. But make sure that you initiate only a relaxing activity. Video games, late night TV, reading, and home cleaning act more like stimulants than relaxers. With a relaxing activity, you will usually grow tired within about 30 minutes, at which time you can return to bed and start a restful sleep. Many individuals report that prayer and praise act as the best possible sleep aids. A few individuals feel guilty about falling asleep while praying, but God understands our need for sleep. I would rather fall asleep while talking to God than abuse my body with insomnia.

Get up and go to bed at the same time every day, even on weekends and during vacation. This trains your body and mind to sleep and awake at consistent times of the day.

Avoid naps—if you have a sleep problem. Instead, teach your body to expect sleep whenever you go to bed at nighttime.

Avoid bright lights at night. Light stimulates the brain into thinking that it is daytime. Within the last hour before bedtime, use dim lights.

Avoid discussing problems during the late evening. Conflict and tension stimulate the brain and prevent sleep. As adults, we can save these issues to discuss the next day either in the morning, or immediately after we arrive home from work.

Avoid heavy meals within the last two hours of bedtime. As your body digests food, it usually keeps you awake

Avoid strenuous exercise within three hours before bedtime. Exercise releases endorphins that keep you awake. Schedule your exercise routine early enough to avoid interfering with sleep.

When all else fails, **ask your physician about taking melatonin**. If he or she approves, start with a low dose (3 mg) and increase as you find that you need more. Adults usually produce less melatonin as they age. Many retirement age adults find that they need a small dose of melatonin as a nightly supplement.

Exercise 5-1: Using the suggestions above, what are your personal plans for promoting good sleep hygiene?

CHAPTER 6

Physical Resilience by Aerobic Exercise

Exercise—what makes me hate it?

Adam and Eve's story possibly provides meaningful clues about how God designed humankind. Genesis 2:15 (NIV) states, "The Lord God took the man and put him in the Garden of Eden to work it and take care of it." From this verse, we assume that God ordained all mankind to work, and that Adam and Eve spent their days working in the Garden. The Bible never mentions explicitly what the work included, but gardening usually includes strenuous tasks such as pruning, digging and lifting. When not working in the garden, they probably spent the other parts of their day gathering (picking, cutting, digging, and carrying) food to eat. Since the Bible never mentions any other occupation, we assume they probably worked and exercised almost all day. Until God cursed the ground, they avoided painful toil, but not strenuous exercise. God ordained physical work as the norm in the Garden of Eden.

After their spiritual fall, God says, "Cursed is the ground because of you; through painful toil you will eat of it all the days of your life" (Genesis 3:17, NIV). From that time forward, Adam and Eve worked and exercised with painful toil, and the rest of humankind must follow in their footsteps. Modern anthropologists agree, telling us that prehistoric man probably exercised at the level of today's elite athletes, walking and running in excess of four hours per day. The old adage, "no pain, no gain," applies as much to the lifestyle of ministers today as it applied to Adam and Eve after the "fall."

God ordained exercise as the norm even in the idyllic Garden of Eden and requires strenuous physical activity (and painful toil) as a normal consequence for living in a fallen world.

In contrast to burnout, Jesus says, "Come to me, all you who are weary and burdened, and I will give you rest. Take my yoke upon you and learn from me, for I am gentle and humble in heart, and you will find rest for your souls" (Matthew 11:28-30, NIV). Some individuals assume that "rest for your souls" eliminates the need for physical, painful toil. Although Jesus talks about "rest for your souls," some possibly try to read more into the passage than He says. These individuals would assert that redeemed Christians do not need to worry about "painful toil" because their physical burden lifts along with their spiritual burden. That is, Genesis 3:17 ceases to apply to Christians.

If the curse of "painful toil" vanishes for Christians, why does the other part of the curse—physical death—still apply to Christians and non-Christians alike? To lift the curse of painful toil while retaining a curse of physical death looks like a double standard in reasoning. And, most missionaries quickly realize that pastors in undeveloped regions of the world still suffer from painful toil as much as their unsaved neighbors. In some countries, pastoring a church almost guarantees a substandard, painful existence below the living standard of their non-Christian neighbors. Even in industrialized nations, most farmers quickly point to the ground itself—the ground remains just as hard and grows just as many thorns and weeds for Christian farmers as for non-Christian farmers. The earth remains cursed, and all who live on it still deal with the curse. Regardless of the outlook on the phrase "painful toil," God ordained physical labor as the norm for Adam and Eve even before their spiritual fall. To assume that modern humankind may avoid labor and instead rest in ease may indicate a not-too-subtle acceptance of the prosperity gospel.

> When we choose to avoid God's natural rhythms,
> consequences inevitably result.

In contrast to the rigorous exercise of the primitive societies in the world, only 26 percent of North Americans exercise at a level recommended for physical and mental health (Center for Disease Control and Prevention, 2003). More than half (59 percent) of North Americans engage in no physical exercise at all. The modern office setting for many Christians throughout the world resembles the North American sedentary existence. However, God never designed humankind—fallen or otherwise—for the modern North American sedentary lifestyle. Worse yet, some individuals from the modern industrialized world assume that ignoring Genesis 3:17 confers no consequences.

In North America, the sedentary lifestyle stimulates the highest rates of burnout and depression in the world (Kessler et. al., 2005). The rate of depression in North America soars approximately ten times higher than two generations ago. In contrast, the Amish show the lowest rates of burnout and depression of any people group in North America (Egeland and Hostetter, 1983). However, physical work and exercise characterizes their lifestyle.

Also note the Kaluli (hunter/gatherers) of Papua New Guinea. In spite of their extremely difficult living conditions (possibly similar to what many would consider as painful toil), they rarely show any sign of depression. Thus, avoidance of exercise seems to leave humans significantly susceptible to depression (Penedo and Dahn, 2005; U.S. Department of Health and Human Services, 1999).

Exercise—what makes it so difficult?

Ministers in the early 1900s exercised as a normal routine in their daily life. They walked great distances between towns and cities, labored to construct their homes, hauled water from the well, raised animals to eat, carried food home from the local market, and often even made their own clothes and washed them by hand. In contrast, modern missionaries fly in an airplane, drive an agency-owned automobile, and prepare Bible school lectures and newsletter articles while sitting at an office desk. Pastors and missionaries live extremely stressful lives. Yet, many find that exercise in a modern world remains a difficult choice.

The ministerial lifestyle sometimes inhibits exercise. In many cities and countries, sidewalks either don't exist or so many people fill them that a brisk walk or jog is out of the question. In other countries, jogging on a public street invites robbery or death by a vehicular accident. In many industrialized countries, the culture promotes a sedentary lifestyle in which a minister sits at an office desk, commutes to work by automobile, and returns to a walled compound with many of the conveniences of a modern society. Somehow, this modern sedentary lifestyle seems the antithesis of the painful toil and physical labor mentioned in Genesis 3:17.

What keeps ministers from exercising? I've heard a long list of excuses. Stephen Ilardi (*The Depression Cure*) states that it boils down to this—exercise is *hard* work. When we exercise only for the sake of health, exercise feels like toil. God said mankind would toil, and toiling (exercising when we don't feel like it) feels unpleasant. However, toiling remains part of the curse, and God states that it will even feel "painful."

Ilardi notes that prehistoric humankind (especially after Adam and Eve departed the garden) never needed to *try* to exercise. That is, they didn't need a treadmill to maintain fitness. To survive, they *had* to exercise. They survived day after day by toiling, often painfully. The curse extended throughout their life. When farming made food a little more plentiful, they almost certainly avoided exercise in their spare time. They probably conserved their reserve energy for the next crop planting or the next hunt, rather than jumping on the equivalent of a treadmill.

Indeed, the Bible refers to humankind's efforts to gather food, raise crops, herd animals, hunt, and work. But it never mentions the need for a treadmill. If we gave Adam, Noah, King David, or even Jesus a treadmill, they would certainly laugh at the thought of *needing* to get additional exercise. Ilardi notes that when we see a treadmill, our first thought says, "Don't get on that machine. That thing isn't going anywhere. It has no purpose. Save your energy for the next crop planting or the next hunt." Regardless, God expects us to labor (exercise).

For Christians in industrialized societies, the avoidance of exercise perhaps represents the most overlooked source of synchronization. The same principle holds true for middle class Christians in non-industrialized societies.

In contrast to the culture of Adam and Eve, industrialized societies make exercise *seem* like an option. Some even view exercise as archaic as the word "toil." Few Christians choose to toil, physically. How many more especially try to avoid the *painful* toil? Possibly, most Christians no longer believe the curse. They would say, "This applies only to Adam and Eve, certainly not to me. I'm a missionary, or an evangelist, or a computer scientist, or a redeemed saint!"

Some ministers discuss their fear of synchritization. That is, they fear the potential of unwittingly synchritizing their Christian values with the surrounding culture.

A few ministers suffer burnout and depression in spite of regular exercise. In my experience, however, they represent a rare exception. Although regular exercise may rarely fail to prevent burnout and depression, those who experience burnout and depression subsequently avoid regular exercise (Seligman, 1990; Penedo and Dahn, 2005; U.S. Department of Health and Human Services, 1999).

Exercise—how do I know that it is good?

First of all, God ordained strenuous physical activity as the norm for fallen humankind. That alone represents enough reason to for me as a minister to choose this activity even when I dislike it. However, recent secular research on burnout shows that exercise provides a benefit equivalent to cognitive therapy (Fremont & Craighead, 1987), and antidepressants (Blumenthal et al, 1999, 2008). It also lowers the rate of relapse compared to other interventions (Babyak et al, 2000) and reduces the risk of depression (e.g. Ross & Hayes, 1988). Suffice to say, whatever God ordains is good—even when it feels painful.

A study from the Copenhagen City Heart Study showed that Going for a jog regularly affects your longevity. Women who regularly jogged lived 5.6 years longer than women who didn't, and men who jogged lived 6.2 years longer than those who didn't.

The study looked at 20,000 people and assessed the mortality rates of 1,116 male joggers and 762 female joggers with the non-joggers. The results showed that over 35 years, the risk of dying over the course of the study was reduced by 44 percent for joggers.

Exercise—how much is a good thing?

Due to God's mandate, this question remained irrelevant throughout most of history. Exercise became a choice for the first time in the later part of the 20th century. In much of the world it remains a choice in the 21st century.

Check with your doctor before beginning a new fitness program to determine your ability to exercise. To prevent burnout and depression, Stephen Ilardi (2009) recommends 30 minutes of aerobic exercise three times a week. He recommends meeting with an exercise consultant for the first six weeks.

Aerobic Range			
Age	70% Maximum Heart Rate	80% Maximum Heart Rate	90% Maximum Heart Rate	100% Maximum Heart
20-24	140	160	180	200
25-29	137	156	176	195
30-34	133	148	171	190
34-39	130	144	166	185
40-44	126	139	162	180
45-49	122	136	156	174
50-54	119	132	153	170
55-59	116	128	149	165
60-64	112	124	144	160
65-69	109	124	140	155
70+	105	120	135	150

Exercise 6-1: If you feel able to exercise, find an aerobic exercise in which your heart rate remains within the range shown in the table above. Start at a level no higher than the 70 percent maximum heart rate (see second column above). Try to maintain yourself at the 70

percent level for 30 minutes. If you can't talk with some difficulty while maintaining the 70 percent heart rate, then back off to the next level shown for someone who is slightly older than yourself. Keep backing down to the next level for someone slightly older than yourself until you find a heart rate at which you can talk with some difficulty while maintaining the exercise for about 30 minutes. When your endurance increases enough that the 70 percent level feels comfortable, gradually move up to the 80 percent level. Proceed to the 90 percent level only after the 80 percent level feels comfortable. Proceed to the 100 percent level only with approval from your physician.

Exercise—what motivates us?

Humankind naturally tries to avoid exercise (especially painful toil). Thus, no known clay tablets or prehistoric writings record the development of treadmills or any other exercise equipment. Trudging to a nearby gym on a regular basis may seem like a far cry from the Garden of Eden. Stephen Ilardi (p.117) notes, "… we're designed to avoid extra physical activity—but what about necessary activity?"

Like prehistoric humankind on a deer hunt, when we possess a clear goal or purpose the activity seems easier, if not enjoyable. He notes, "… whenever we're caught up in enjoyable meaningful activity, our tolerance for exercise goes up dramatically." Thus, he urges us to make our workouts as purposeful as possible. For instance, defeating your coworker in a game of table tennis seems more interesting than pedaling an exercise bike; jogging through scenic countryside seems more exhilarating than jogging on a treadmill; dancing in your living room with your spouse seems more enticing than lifting weights; and jogging with a friend seems more interesting than jogging on a treadmill.

Brainstorm ways to build purpose into your exercise routine. Thus, exercising with great music seems much more enjoyable than exercising in silence. Likewise, listening to an audio-book or taped sermon makes exercise more enjoyable than exercising without purposeful thought. One word of caution—avoid using anything that might impair your ability to hear traffic while jogging on a street.

Often, a social purpose motives exercise. Thus, walking with someone else lifts the mood more than exercising alone. Ilardi notes (p. 126), "The latest research suggests that exercising with others may be more effective in fighting depression than working out alone." Even when the social contact comes from an exercise coach, the coach provides purpose and direction. Some individuals search for a dog (canine) as a regular workout companion. Pets also enjoy exercise as long as it occurs with the one they love.

If pre-historic humans didn't exercise just for the sake of exercise, you probably won't either. When you pair the exercise with an enjoyable activity like one of those listed below, or with an individual with whom you enjoy fellowship, your motivation to exercise will soar.

Ilardi also recommends finding at least three aerobic activities. As the climate, workload, or location changes, you can easily transition from one exercise activity to another. If you choose only one activity, you may eventually feel bored and quit altogether. Worse yet, any change in climate, workload or travel can easily torpedo your exercise routine. Walking satisfies many individuals, especially when they can walk with a friend or spouse. However, broaden your activities to include more choices than walking.

Consider outdoor activities (only in safe locations) such as:

Walking	Skating or skiing
Golf (when walking at	Hiking
a brisk rate)	Climbing
Jogging	Yard work
Swimming	Home remodeling
Cycling	

Consider competitive sports (especially indoor) such as:

Basketball	Racquetball or handball
Soccer	Badminton
Tennis or table tennis	Volleyball

Consider activities in a gym such as:

Exercise machines	Weight lifting
(treadmill, row	Self-defense class
machine, stair-step	Aerobics class
machine, cycling)	

Exercise 6-2: List three aerobic activities that you can pursue at different times of the year. What is your plan to pursue them?

Exercise 6-3: Find an exercise accountability partner. An accountability partner will usually provide a meaningful nudge to get you started. And, you will, in turn, provide that same nudge to your partner. That is, your accountability partner needs you as much as you need him or her. List two individuals who might serve as your accountability partners.

Exercise—when and how long?

As soon as you identify an exercise, write out a schedule that includes when to start and stop and a weekly routine that provides for exercise at evenly spaced intervals throughout the week. Dr. Cooper, in *Faith Based Fitness* says, "Your schedule will never magically 'open up' unless you understand that your basic faith demands that you take good care of your body. And that means making a firm commitment that will get you off your backside and launch you on a life-changing program." At least three times per week, try to set aside at least one hour to change clothes, exercise, shower afterward, and cool down. Since exercise pumps endorphins into the blood, exercise inhibits sleep until the endorphins dissipate—about three hours. Therefore, try to finish exercising at least three hours before bedtime.

A lifestyle that includes daily exercise offers many benefits for physical, emotional, and spiritual health. Ministers, even more than other members of the secular society, struggle with depression. Two common depression symptoms—lack of energy and lack of concentration—make it challenging to maintain a consistent devotional life. This spiritual deficit leads to a deep sense of guilt. Moderate exercise can break this vicious cycle. In addition to preventing depression, exercise provides the following dividends:

Energy. Exercise unlocks energy. Even a half-hour workout or a quick walk around the block will provide you with an extra lift and the ability to stay focused throughout a busy day.

Weight Control. A trip to the health club results in calories burned. Calories burned equals weight loss. Research indicates that a healthy dose of physical exercise suppresses the appetite, helping you to curb the urge to reach for that second helping, extra candy bar, or piece of cake.

Sense of Well-being. Extended physical activity causes the brain to release endorphins. These chemicals reduce stress and anxiety and promote feelings of peacefulness. Exercise almost always lifts the mood.

Financial Savings. Yes, it's true! If you exercise, clothes will fit properly and last longer. Preventative health efforts also pay off in money saved on medications and health care charges.

Restful Sleep. People who engage in sports or physical activity savor the effects of sound slumber. With less anxiety, sleep is undisturbed and restorative. Better rest results in higher productivity and contentedness. However, try to finish your exercise routine at least three hours before bedtime.

If you find yourself the least bit ambivalent about exercise, we highly recommend *Faith-based Fitness: The Medical Program That Uses Spiritual Motivation To Achieve Maximum Health And Add Years To Your Life*, by Dr. Kenneth Cooper. His book helps Christians to build motivation for setting up and maintaining a reasonable exercise program.

CHAPTER 7

Physical Resilience by Sunlight

No one needed to prompt Adam and Eve to get outdoors into the sunlight. They spent their daylight hours working outdoors in the garden. The Scriptures never mention how many hours they spent outdoors, but since they lived as gardeners, they probably spent almost all of their waking hours outdoors. And for the centuries following, men hunted and women gathered—outdoors. For most primitive cultures, inadequate sun exposure seemed virtually impossible. Even as little as one hundred years ago, most individuals worked outdoors.

The need for sunlight

Serotonin serves as a primary brain chemical. Serotonin transmits signals between all the brain neurons. So without adequate serotonin, the brain slows down. The Bible calls it a downcast spirit. The medical profession calls it "depression." Thus chemically, depression is little more than an inadequate supply of serotonin. Fortunately, bright light stimulates the brain to produce serotonin. Some individuals assume that a daily dose of vitamin D substitutes for sunlight. While vitamin D provides an essential chemical for skin health and for other purposes, it never substitutes for the effect of sunlight. Sunlight stimulates the brain to produce serotonin. Vitamin D never affects serotonin levels.

How much sunlight did Adam and Eve get each day?

Although Scriptures avoid discussing these minute details, we can infer much from them. Since Adam and Even spent all day working in the Garden, we can assume that they probably spent eight or more hours outdoors each day. Modern anthropologists indicate that even after they left the Garden, humankind probably spend most of their day hunting and gathering outdoors. Thus, they easily got an adequate amount of sunlight.

Seasonal Affective Disorder (SAD)

In northern climates and climates near the South Pole, the earth's tilt limits sunlight during the winter months. In these climates, some individuals succumb to Seasonal Affective Disorder (SAD). SAD is a depression induced by inadequate sunlight during the darkest months of the year. Thus, the depression rate soars during winter months. However, many cities with high levels of air pollution also suffer from a lack of sunlight. In these cities, the pollution and chronically smoggy winter weather further blocks the sunlight. In China, Egypt, Indonesia and many developing countries, air pollution may limit visibility to less than a few hundred feet. Even on a cloudless day, minimal sunlight reaches the ground. In these countries, the sunlight level sometimes barely exceeds the level of artificial indoor lighting.

Please access the playlist referenced on page 31, and view the video titled "Seasonal Affective Disorder" to better understand this common problem.

How much sunlight do you get each day?

In modern cultures, however, the majority of working people spend their time working indoors. Most ministers work indoors, and most of their offices provide adequate lighting for reading—about 100 lumens of light. Outdoors, the sun provides between 10,000 and 100,000 lumens, 100 to 1000 times brighter than indoors. Even 24 hours of indoor lighting barely provides the equivalent of ten minutes outdoors, and how many individuals sleep with all their lights on? Thus, many ministers fail to get adequate sunlight. Due to insufficient bright sunlight in their environment, their brain fails to produce a sufficient supply of serotonin.

Fortunately, very little light is needed to produce an adequate supply of serotonin. Usually, as little as 30 minutes of 10,000 ft. Lambert light (direct sunlight) triggers the brain to start producing serotonin.

So, how can we intentionally find enough sun to provide health and productivity? Remember that you may wear sunscreen and appropriate clothing; only your eyes need exposure.

- Take a walk during your lunch break.
- Remove your sunglasses for at least thirty minutes each day so that the eye's pupil will receive sun rays. (Avoid directly staring at the sun.)
- Abandon the car for short errands, and choose to walk.
- Walk the dog.
- Play out of doors: tennis, golf, basketball, bike riding, etc. Especially on your Sabbath Day, make sure that you incorporate some type of outdoor recreation.
- Enjoy some time in your garden . . . working and walking with your Creator.
- Purchase a light box. For individuals who suffer from seasonal affective disorder, a light box provides an especially important source of sunlight. Light boxes are available online for as little as $170 and will provide the necessary 10,000 lux

of broadband light. Avoid the cheaper light boxes under $150. They are generally too small to provide adequate light. Some types of bulbs flicker. Look for one with flicker-free technology such as the Day-Light DL930 by Uplift Technologies. The Caribbean Sun Box available at www.caribbeansunbox.org (see photo below) offers another high quality option based on LED technology. Most LED light boxes operate on both 110 volt and 220 volt current. Also note that a bright light can aggravate a few medical

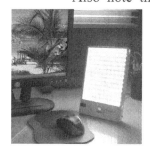

problems. Check with your doctor if you suffer from macular degeneration, bipolar disorder, or any eye problems. For those with extremely sensitive eyes, some companies produce light boxes that use blue light. For more information on sun boxes, please access the playlist referenced on page 31, and then view the video titled "Sunbox SAD Voice of America."

Protection from sunlight

Susceptibility to skin cancer plagues some individuals, especially those with a fair skin color. If your skin is fair, make sure to protect it with clothing or sun-block. Although you need sunlight to produce serotonin, the sun merely needs to shine on your eyes, not the rest of your skin. Make sure you get adequate sunlight, but protect your skin from cancer.

Exercise 7-1: Using the suggestions above, what are your personal plans for obtaining adequate sunlight on a daily basis?

CHAPTER 8

Physical Resilience by Omega-3 Food

God designed the Garden of Eden with a wide variety of wholesome nutritious foods. So what did Adam and Eve eat? And what about the diet of other biblical characters like Noah?

Genesis 9:3 (NIV) relates God's provision for Noah, "Everything that lives and moves will be food for you. Just as I gave you the green plants, I now give you everything."

Before the flood, humankind existed on plants and vegetables. After the flood, God gave permission to consume plants, vegetables, and animals. Unfortunately a lot of modern food products seem quite different from "the Garden" variety that God designed for Adam and Eve and even for Noah.

The need for omega-3 fatty acids

Serotonin serves as a primary brain chemical that transmits signals throughout the brain. Omega-3 fatty acids provide a molecular building block for serotonin and stimulate the production of anti-inflammatory hormones. Omega-3 provides good food for the brain. Hibbeln (1998) found a strong inverse correlation between omega-3s consumed and the rate of burnout and depression. Peet and Horrobin (2001) confirmed that depressed patients have low plasma level of omega-3s. So without enough omega-3, an individual develops heightened susceptibility to burnout and depression.

Omega-3s come from fish (especially oily fish), some green vegetables, and olive oil. In contrast, omega-6 seems to bind the enzymes needed to process omega-3. Additionally, omega-6 increases inflammation and increases cortisol, an inflammatory stress hormone. Thus, a diet high in omega-6 restricts one's ability to use omega-3.

Menu from the Heart Attack Grill

Omega-6 comes from grain-fed meat, fried food (especially fast food such as hamburgers and French fries), snack chips, baked goods, and seed based oils (canola, sunflower, corn, and vegetable). Just like grain-fed humans, grain-fed animals also exhibit high levels of omega-6. Of all the foods consumed in industrialized nations, seed-based flour, vegetable oils, grain-fed livestock, grain-fed poultry, and grain-fed farm fish probably account for the majority of the omega-6 consumed. Individuals living in primitive societies (such as the tribes in Papua New Guinea and the Aborigine of Australia) usually consume range-fed and wild animals instead of grain-fed animals, and fresh fruit and vegetables instead of deep-fried foods. And they generally show blood levels close to a 1:1 ratio of omega-3 to omega-6. North Americans generally show a

16:1 ratio of omega-6 to omega-3 in their blood. Increasingly, other cultures show a similar ratio.

Since Adam and Eve existed without processed foods and seed-based cooking oils, they probably had the ideal 1:1 ratio of omega-3 to omega-6. Since Noah consumed range-fed and wild animals (in contrast to grain-fed livestock), he also probably had the ideal 1:1 ratio of omega-3 to omega-6. Japan is the only industrialized nation where individuals commonly consume a 1:1 ratio of omega-3 to omega-6 fatty acids. However, the Japanese consume miniscule amounts of beef and typically eat fish three times a day. From all indications, God never designed anyone to live on the modern North American fast-food diet, or even the grain-fed and processed meat products available in most industrialized nations.

If you consume grain-fed meat (including beef, pork, and farm-raised fish) fried food, snack chips, baked goods, or seed-based oils (canola, sunflower, corn, and vegetable), you possibly consume an unhealthy ratio of omega-3 to omega-6. Due to the effects of the modern diet, the majority of people all over the world (excluding Japan) need to supplement their diet with omega-3.

In *Defense of Food*, Michael Pollan relates an interesting insight into the importance of diet and omega-3. He tells a story in which ten Australian Aborigines switched from their hunter-gatherer lifestyle to adopt the Western diet. Within a year, all of them developed diabetes and other inflammation-linked disorders. Fortunately, a diet researcher convinced them to return to their Aborigine diet of seafood, kangaroos, insect larvae, and wild plants. Within two months, their general health and diabetes condition significantly improved. And blood samples showed a significant change in their ratio of omega-3 to omega-6.

Adopting a healthy diet in a foreign culture poses significant problems. Low-cost cooking oil (such as canola oil, sunflower oil, and corn oil) is now available in almost all developing nations. So people in many countries seem to increasingly stir-fry or deep-fry their food. Third world cultures depend on social ties that often center around communal meals. To serve the spiritual needs of those he or she serves means that a missionary will consume unhealthy food and even learn to enjoy it. Likewise, many other ministers live in subcultures in which they consume fried catfish, fried hash-browns, grits, hamburgers, and biscuits with gravy.

Thus modern technology sometimes promotes an unhealthy diet. However, alternatives remain available if we choose them. Usually a single 1,000 mg tablet of an omega-3 supplement will return you reasonably close to a healthy 1:1 balance. For most ministers, this offers a low-cost and culturally acceptable alternative to an inherently unhealthy diet. A daily omega-3 supplement is reasonably cheap, available at many pharmacies, and easily ordered through the Internet.

Some people complain that omega-3 supplements cause a nasty fish breath. Unfortunately, fish decays fairly quickly in a warm room. When processed shoddily, omega-3 supplements can smell fishy and even upset the stomach. If you decide to purchase an omega-3 supplement, we recommend avoiding cheap products. The better quality (and slightly higher priced) supplements rarely result in a fish breath. We recommend purchasing only molecularly distilled omega-3 supplements. Since omega-3 comes from fish liver and since fish liver filters toxins, non-molecularly distilled omega-3 sometimes includes traces of these toxins. The trace toxins may or may not affect you. However, the molecularly distilled omega-3 costs only a fraction more than its cheaper counterpart and avoids the side affect of a fishy breath. At the time of this writing, the molecularly distilled Mega EFA™ from Neutraceutical Sciences Institute is available online at www.vitacost.com and costs less than many non-distilled and lower quality varieties.

To reduce any taste of fish, try keeping your Omega-3 tablets in the freezer until time to take them. Refrigeration becomes especially important in the warm summer months.

The need for antioxidants

In *The Depression Cure* (2009) Stephen Ilardi states:

As mentioned, fish oil and oxygen don't mix: the oxygen spoils it. And we all have some harmful forms of oxygen in our bodies, carried around by dangerous molecules call free radicals. These molecules can damage any fish oil you consume just as soon as it hits the bloodstream, making the omega-3s less useful to your brain. Luckily, antioxidants—nutrients like Vitamin C—can protect omega-3s from such damage.

To ensure that you have enough antioxidants in your system, it's advisable to take a daily multivitamin, in addition to a vitamin C supplement at a daily dose of 500 mg.

Exercise 8-1: From where will you obtain a daily dose of at least 1000mg of Omega-3?

How to get started

For training in how to eat God's way, ask these questions: How close is this food to the way God created it? Is this animal fed grain, hormones, or is it allowed to graze on the open range in the way God designed? Is this a refined food or one that is full of preservatives? Does it include additives such as salt, sugar, or high-fructose corn syrup? Is it hydrogenated?

When shopping for food items, you might consider noticing how far each item has evolved from its "original" God-given packaging. Generally the more processes required to bring food to the supermarket shelf, the less value it brings to one's health.

Plan meals that are low in saturated and trans-saturated fat and high in fiber. Small amounts of lean beef, chicken, pork, and fish—along with vegetables and fruit—offer endless possibilities for nutritious recipes.

Include items high in omega-3. These include fish (salmon, mackerel, halibut, sardines, tuna, and herring) and walnuts.

Use moderation with foods such as coffee, soft drinks, and rich desserts.

Enjoy a variety of foods, but control food portions. For these guidelines, we look to the residents of Okinawa, known as the longest-living people in the world. The Okinawa diet emphasizes eating well but less. Three principles are summed up in the following three phrases: kuten gwa (eating small portions); hara hachi hu (eating until you are 80 percent full); and nuchi gusui (eating food for its health value).

Sit down at the table, enjoy the aroma, and savor each bite. Slowing down aids the digestive system and helps you to control food consumption. The Okinawans decided that it is ideal to stop eating a little before one feels full (around 80 percent). The best way to make this happen is to sit down, eat slowly, and enjoy being with your family, friends, and Heavenly Father.

Consider menu planning, grocery shopping, and meal preparation as a spiritual act. A healthy body allows the mind to respond more readily to the voice of God and provides energy to faithfully obey His call.

Stephen Ilardi (2009) offers the following suggestions:

- Switch to grass-fed beef, or simply drop beef from you diet altogether.
- Stick mostly with lean meats like chicken breast and fish.
- Stay away from fried foods (and most fast food in general).
- Cook with olive oil or coconut oil (fruit-based oils), and avoid seed-based oils like soybean oil, corn oil, canola oil, and sunflower oil. Use seed-based oil for salad dressing.
- Use butter instead of margarine.
- Avoid snack chips and baked goods.
- Start reading product labels, and stay away from foods that contain lots of seed-based oils (there are thousands of them).

PART III:

How to Build

Emotional Resilience

Emotional resilience—what is it?

To a large extent, hope determines emotional resilience. Without hope, we feel despair and give up. With hope, we persevered in spite of stressors. Many individuals build emotional resilience that almost inherently pull them through a crisis. Others, especially ministers, tend to neglect building factors that preserve and enhance hope. The six chapters of Part III describe methods to build and preserve hope.

Emotional Resilience Assessment

Please score the below items as a 0, 1, 3, or 5, indicating the degree to which the statement characterizes you.

0 = this almost never characterizes me.

1 = this characterizes me a little.

3 = this characterizes me somewhat.

5 = this characterizes me quite a bit.

Assessment A

	I talk deeply with at least one close friend.
	When I think about myself, I feel good about what I have become.
	I pursue clear goals toward ministry.
	I pursue an intentional plan to improve my family relationships.
	I pursue personal leisure time away from ministry.
	I pursue personal interests other than ministry.
	I pursue clear goals to promote my health and fitness.
	I am constantly trying to learn more about how to do ministry better.

_____ Total A Score

Assessment B

	I worry a lot.
	I have a hard time letting go of past hurts.
	I work too much.
	I still think about work projects even while I am socializing with others.
	A lot of my goals never get accomplished.

_____ Total B Score

The following emotional factors build hope and hardiness (emotional resilience) against the effects of life's stressors:

- Socialization
- Reversing rumination
- Self-esteem
- Well balanced personal goals
- Attainable ministry goals
- Goal refinement skills

How to score your physical resilience self-assessment

Total the scores of your assessment A items to find your Total A Score. Total the scores of your assessment B items to find your Total B Score. Subtract your Total B Score from your Total A Score to obtain your Emotional Resilience Score.

Total A Score - Total B Score = Emotional Resilience Score

If your emotional resilience score is:

0-19 = Your emotional resilience is seriously degraded. You are highly susceptible to burnout. You can benefit from this section.

20-30 = Your emotional resilience is marginal. Only one or two crises may stimulate burnout. You can benefit from some chapters in this section.

31-40 = Your emotional resilience is fairly good at this time. Please read the following chapters to better understand how to keep yourself emotionally resilient.

For additional information on these emotional factors, please see:

Emmons, R.A.. *The psychology of ultimate concerns*. New York: Guilford Press, 1999.

Ilardi, S. S. *The Depression Cure: the 6-step program to beat depression without drugs*. DaCapo Press: Cambridge MA., 2009.

Seigman, M. E. P. *Authentic Happiness*. New York: Free Press, 2002.

Schiraldi, Glenn R. *Building Self-Esteem: A 125 Day Program*. Ellicott City MD: Chevron Publishing Corp., 1993.

Snyder, C. R. *Handbook of Hope: Theory, Measures, & Applications*. San Diego, CA: Academic Press, 2002.

CHAPTER 9

Emotional Resilience With Socialization

What makes socialization important?

When humans socialize at a deep level, the socialization stimulates the brain to start producing serotonin. And serotonin provides an important margin against burnout and depression. So socialization offers more than a "nice" activity. Socialization provides a chemical jolt to the brain that physically protects humans from depression.

When asked what makes their lives most meaningful, most individuals first refer to their social relationships (Fehr, 4). For Christians in particular, relationships with God, self, and others form the basis for all meaningfulness. Relationships represent the only earthly possessions that we can take with us to heaven.

In Romans, the Apostle Paul reminded Christians to value relationships when he wrote, "So in Christ we who are many form one body, and each member belongs to all the others" (Rom. 12:5).

Unlike secular society, good relationships not only enhance Christian life, they form the fundamental fabric of spiritual maturity. Consider Abraham. He matured spiritually, but not by reading God's Word—the written Word did not yet exist. His relationships with God, self and others determined his spiritual maturity.

The Christian life not only rests on the development of relationships with God, self and others, but God created us to have relationships.

Socialization within a small, tight network (a tribe) seems as old as the Israelites. From the time of Jacob, the Israelites united in small tribes, facing together a world hostile to pursuing the one true God. In Leviticus, God commanded them to form social networks around the tabernacle and avoid intermarriage (socialization) with unbelievers. When they invaded Canaan, God not only instructed them to avoid socialization with outsiders, but they settled in Canaan by tribe. No Israelite survived apart from their group. The tribe formed their basic identity.

This clannish togetherness still characterizes many cultures. These groups normally prohibit privacy. As we travel in South America, Asia, and Eurasia, we commonly find several generations of families living within the same house, often in the same room. To the horror of Westerners, these totally enmeshed social networks control almost everything that happens within each family, and often within each community. The clan spends nearly all day every day with each other.

A few Western psychologists point to enmeshment as a hallmark of mental illness. However, Westerners show over ten times the amount of mental illness compared to these enmeshed cultures. And modern psychologists are just now beginning to understand the power and health of deep socialization.

For the most part, socialization looks entirely different in North

America than in the rest of the world. North Americans tend to work, eat, drive to work, sleep, and "crash" at home to recreate alone, or watch an unresponsive television (instead of socializing). Compared to most other cultures, North Americans rarely invite others into their home for dinner, or recreate with their neighbors. Almost 25% of North Americans state that they have NO intimate friends, and about half state that they have no friends on which they can rely. Compared to peoples in most other cultures, most North Americans lead a relatively isolated life.

When our career gets in the way of our vocation,
we burn out and lose both.

The opposite of socialization (isolation) forms the basis of depression and burnout. With even a mild depression, the victim starts to withdraw from socialization. Thus, isolation stimulates depression which stimulates further isolation which stimulates further depression, and so on. Thus, isolation (the lack of socialization) stimulates a downward cycle of depression and burnout.

How does social isolation affect ministry?

Some ministers live as if they value ministry more than people. They spend increasingly long hours in ministry, consumed by pursuit of a successful ministry, even while they spend less time connecting deeply with people. For instance:

- How many wives spend most of their day home schooling their children (their ministry) while neglecting time to connect deeply with their friends?
- How many ministers spend most of their day developing a new ministry program (e.g. developing a radio program, developing a new training course, developing new skills for ministry, studying the Bible, or developing new sermons)

while neglecting to develop friendships?

- How many ministers neglect or even sever thier ties with close friends to pursue "the ministry?"

Many Christians, world-wide, spend so much time listening to the one-way dialog of a TV that they neglect sharpening their ability to engage in a two-way dialog with people. I rediscovered this point recently when I visited a childhood friend and his wife. Over a two-hour dinner together, I asked question after question about their lives and their hopes and dreams. They seemed to relish talking about their career accomplishments and plans for future accomplishments. And I enjoyed listening to their story. During this time, however, they never asked a single question about me or my family. As I departed, I realized that they seemed to value only themselves. Since a one-way dialog of a TV defined their social life at home, I'm unsure that they knew how to engage in a two-way dialog.

Likewise, I find the same problem in many countries outside North America. Frequently, children and adults alike watch TV in the relative seclusion of their bedroom, while fewer dialogs occur between family members. Their relationships resemble the one-way dialog of a TV in which they can either play the role of the TV or they play the role of the listener, but their skills at a two-way dialog grow increasingly weaker.

How can a minister develop a healthy amount of socialization?

For ministers, this raises some even more difficult questions:

- Who's available for socialization when you live in a different country than your birth country?
- Should I focus more on friends within my church or friends back in my home town?
- How do I socialize with those of different cultures?

- What should I do when my friends (or fellow ministers) criticize me?
- Should I socialize with my coworkers? Isn't it a conflict of interest?
- How can I socialize when I'm already burned out?

Who's available for socialization when you live in a country different than your birth country? This question is often an excuse to avoid socialization. Of course, it takes lots of work to develop new friends, especially when the options are reduced. But are the options really reduced, or are the options simply different?

Many third world cities offer an international church. Ilardi states, "Nothing binds people together more effectively than a shared purpose and a set of common goals." Especially if you have no other options, try the available international church. Flex a little with new ecumenical approaches. Keep in mind that church members need your socialization as much as you need theirs.

Volunteer for organizations that help the homeless and even consider a Non-Government Organization (NGO). You may not appreciate some of their values, but regardless their differences, you still need social interaction.

Look on the internet for special interest groups. These groups bring individuals together who share common interests. The fact that you are 10,000 miles away seldom matters on the internet. Write and send photos to those with similar interests.

Join self-help groups through the internet. Perhaps it is the search for intimacy and friendships that draws large numbers of people to internet forums such as MySpace and Facebook. These venues offer great potential for connecting with others, including reconnecting with past friends. When the connection occurs through a public media (such as writing on someone's public "wall") most individuals fear the risk of self-disclosure. We encourage you to implement almost any media to initiate a surface relationship. However, a private media, including e-mail or face-to-face communication, usually fosters deeper self-disclosure than a public media.

Abandon the myth that it is impossible to meet and develop close friends. Willing individuals almost always exist who would like to become friends. They are simply different than you.

Developing a friendship takes lots of hard work and may not be easy. Healthy relationships usually require a significant investment of time. Regardless the work, your relationships ensure your emotional health.

How many friends do I need? Some individuals feel much more inhibited, timid, and introverted than others. These individuals often desire deep intimacy, but they limit their efforts to only one or two close friends. While their desire for intimacy offers emotional strength, their restricted outreach to others limits their number of confidants. When these few confidants go on furlough or move away, the introvert often lacks emotional resilience, which can lead to loneliness and depression. Thus, a wide network of friends increases emotional stability. Regardless of your personality, we invite you to intentionally develop **at least three close (intimate) friends**.

Snyder (46) states, "Lacking the opportunity to share our personal experiences dampens, if not completely extinguishes, hopeful thinking." He notes that when we lack friends, we lack the opportunity to share. When we lack the opportunity to share, we lack hope. When we lack hope, we feel depressed. The downward spiral into depression often starts with the lack of friends with whom we can share freely.

Should I focus more on friends within my adopted country or friends back in my country of origin? To better answer this question, please list all the individuals with whom you feel the closest, no matter how far away they happen to live from you (college friends, relatives, coworkers, childhood friends, ministry colleagues, etc.):

-
-
-
-

For most missionaries, many of their closest friends live thousands of miles away, either in their home country or more often, in other countries. Unfortunately, some missionaries rarely contact these friends in spite of their close relationship. We seem to let a geographical separation get in the way of maintaining a close friendship with those most important to us. However, things could be quite different. With modern technology, we can now maintain friendships and even deepen them regardless the physical separation. Missionaries have access to telephone over the internet at reasonable rates. Many can use telephone with video which increases the feeling of connectedness.

We sometimes fail to maintain relationships because we place ministry over people. Those who maintain relationships well simply include telephone and video time as a normal part of their weekly schedule. When (day of the week, and time of the day) can you call each of your friends, given the time difference?

-
-
-
-

How well do I socialize with local individuals? In many cultures, intimacy requires some degree of enmeshment. You may need to discard some of your independent lifestyle.

Regardless, intimacy requires a foundation of trust, and trust develops through appropriate self-disclosure. Matsushima, Rumi, Shiomi, Kunio (2001) found that hesitancy toward personal or private self-disclosure increases loneliness. Since self-disclosure promotes intimacy, anyone who shuns self-disclosure can expect loneliness. Although intimacy requires self-disclosure, self-disclosure fails to produce intimacy, in and of itself.

The truth about self-disclosure is:

- Self-disclosure mutually influences a relationship.
- Self-disclosure is a hallmark of a close relationship.
- However, self-disclosure is NOT synonymous with or even equivalent to having a close relationship.

Sharing your thoughts and feelings leads to a healthy relationship; however, self-disclosure inherently includes risk. Therefore, self-disclosure also requires mutual guidelines. Refrain from disclosing anything to immature Christians that they could interpret as ethically or morally questionable.

Is self-disclosure good? The answer is "Yes, sometimes" and "No, sometimes." Self-disclosure includes many benefits. For instance, a study that investigated the follow-up effect of the Three-Mile Island disaster showed that "...having a confidant improved coping with the stressful event represented by the TMI disaster" (Fleming et al., 16). The confidant effect was not only measured by psychological instruments, but was also evident in physiological measures of catecholamines in their body fluids. Similarly, Pennebaker and O'Heeron (231) found that "...the more time that individuals spent talking with someone about the loss of their spouse [when their spouse committed suicide], the less likely they were to experience increased health problems. Pennebaker describes the benefits as follows:

> ...confronting a trauma helps individuals to understand and assimilate the event. By talking or writing about previously inhibited experiences, individuals translate the event into language. Once encoded linguistically, individuals can more readily understand, find meaning in, or attain closure of the experience (Ibid.).

Thus, individuals tend to cope better with life's stressful events when they have friends with whom to confide their problems. Putting your experiences into language helps the brain to better process the experiences and stressors. Ministers generally experience three to five times more stress than the average secular individual. So, most ministers need confidential self-disclosure.

Jourard (1971), Miller, Berg, & Archer (1983), Taylor & Altman (1966) found that for both males and females, self-disclosure is positively related to satisfaction in friendships. Thus, skills to disclose personal facts and feelings play an important role in the success of any friendship.

Self-disclosure stimulates a few rare problems. For instance, self-disclosure may magnify certain unpleasant feelings if one anticipates an upsetting event. Thus, discussions about the death risk with those who also have loved ones in combat, usually heightens their anxiety through a "pressure cooker" effect. Additionally, when a friend validates negative opinions, negative feelings grow even more negative. Consider your audience before self-disclosing problems and negative feelings. Your disclosure could aggravate the stress for both of you. If you find yourself frequently discussing a common negative experience, change the subject. Always limit the amount of time that you will allow negative venting— five minutes generally serves as a maximum healthy length of time. Then, change the subject to something positive.

Joseph DeVito (120) suggests the following helpful guidelines for setting self-disclosure boundaries.

Consider the motivation for self-disclosure. The motivation for healthy self-disclosure must center on a concern for the relationship. Avoid using self-disclosure as a weapon to hurt another individual. For example, an assistant pastor explains to the senior pastor, "The board invited me to serve as pastor before they asked you." More than likely this self-disclosure will strain the relationship between the two pastors. The goal of self-disclosure focuses not on obtaining power or on punishing, but on enhancing openness to interpersonal communication.

The wrong motivation for self-disclosure commonly draws

people together. For instance, subordinates might lament together over their abuses from a common supervisor. Missionaries sometimes fall into this trap and form close friendships based on a common negative experience or a common threat. Such relationships rarely last. After removing the unhealthy factor and while at the same time neglecting to develop mutual interests, little remains upon which to build a relationship. Consider examining your motives before self-disclosing, making sure that the goal of the self-disclosure focuses on improving intimacy (knowledge about each other) rather than discussing a mutually held negative.

Consider the appropriateness of self-disclosure. Self-disclosure usually develops over time. Budding relationships rarely need deep self-disclosure. Take time in self-disclosing, paying attention to the usefulness of the disclosure and the timing of the information. As intimacy develops, self-disclosures become more appropriate. When disclosing negative information, carefully determine whether the information will help or hinder the developing relationship. Generally, disclosure of deep personal information intimidates a new relationship.

The appropriateness of self-disclosure often depends on one's gender. "In particular, women talking to women often disclose more on personal or sensitive topics, express more feelings, and are more emotionally supportive with each other. Men talking to men, other than activities-related issues, tend to avoid self-disclosure (Berlaga, Metts, Petronio, and Marulis, 49)." Thus, when given a choice between doing an activity or just talking with a same-sex friend, more women than men (57% vs. 16%) preferred talking. When men were given a similar choice, more men than women (84% vs. 43%) preferred engaging in an activity over talking (Caldwell and Peplau, 230). Conflict tends to increase more anxiety in males than females. So, some males prefer to avoid all self-disclosure than risk negative self-disclosure.

Consider the disclosures of the other person. Disclosure remains a two-way street. If one person reveals something personal, the recipient usually expects to hear something personal in return. When one person shares too much or too deeply, it will often cause awkwardness or embarrassment on the part of the person hearing the disclosure. Good disclosure takes place in small doses, appropriately allowing each individual to share at his or her own comfort level. Properly sharing intimacies builds strong relationships. However, it requires the careful attention of both participating individuals. As relationships become stronger, disclosure becomes more natural.

Consider the possible burdens that self-disclosure might entail. Before using self-disclosure, examine the consequences of sharing the information. At times, self-disclosures create problems. For example, I (Beth) met a new colleague with whom I shared a lot in common. I looked forward to working with this woman and getting better acquainted. In the first few minutes of our initial conversation, she mentioned that her father committed suicide when she was only ten years old. She went on to explain that she had suffered from the consequences ever since. Because of the timing of the self-disclosure, my friend's tragic story blocked my ability to develop a friendship. Although I felt empathetic toward her, those feelings failed to provide a foundation for a close relationship. It is normal to share your past hurts and disappointments with a friend; however, make sure that you choose the appropriate time.

At the same time, disclosure of personal struggles with a subordinate usually strains the relationship. This kind of disclosure usually leads to distrust and tension. At other times, especially with a negative self-disclosure, one person may relieve his or her guilt by confessing to another, while at the same time leaving a long-lasting trauma with the one hearing the confession. The goal of self-disclosure must always focus on the health and intimacy of the relationship.

Support and reinforce disclosures. When people feel safe in a relationship, disclosure becomes less threatening. After listening to a disclosure, it would be inappropriate to use sarcasm, jokes, or any form of evaluation. At the same time, sharing a similar disclosure of one's own does not serve a good purpose. Support can take place verbally or nonverbally. Sometimes, even a light touch on the arm speaks volumes to emotionally vulnerable individuals.

What should I do when my friends (or other ministers or peers) put me down? Socialization, though usually healthy, may stimulate burnout and depression when it includes put downs and invalidations. Thus, poisonous relationships stimulate serious dysfunctions that block recovery. When you feel like a relationship requires more energy than what you receive, the relationship is usually poisonous. These relationships fall into two categories:

- *Poisonous relationships that remain repairable*. These relationships consume a considerable amount of time in negative thoughts and negative interpretation. Thus, these relationships require rigid limits. For instance, if the other individual feels burned out or depressed, you might need to limit the amount of time spent mulling over negative events. If negative thinking seems common, limit the negative discussion to no more than five minutes per session with the individual. If the other individual consistently expresses negative or explosive sentiments, then severely restrict the amount of time that you spend with them. If you consistently spend time with someone who expresses negative or explosive emotions, you will probably leave each interaction feeling depressed. Set rigid limits to the amount of time that you are willing to spend in negative thoughts.

- *Non-repairable poisonous relationships*. Periodic but consistent abuse characterizes these relationships. Missionaries commonly experience abuse from locals who, in turn, were raised in cultures in which abuse seems the norm. When the missionary desperately wants approval from such ungodly individuals, the local may find himself with emotional power over the missionary. By withdrawing approval, the local finds that he or she can control the missionary. Although it sounds illogical to the secular world, some ministers seek to fulfill their "call" by spending most of their time with individuals who criticize them, act unkind, and actually dislike them. Although ministers commonly feel called to their vocation, when the ratio of validations to invalidations over several years fails to reach a 5:1 ratio, almost all ministers will experience burnout. For good reason, the Apostle Paul says, "Therefore encourage one another and build each other up, just as in fact you are doing" (1 Thess. 5:11). If you minister in an abusive culture, intentionally seek godly sources of validation to counteract the effect of the culture in which you work. This perhaps represents the most significant source of burnout for ministers.

Should I socialize with my coworkers? Isn't it a conflict of interest? Yes, socialize with coworkers and others in the community.

How can I socialize when I'm already burned out?

- *Disclose* information about yourself, especially your need for friendship. If you feel burned out, you probably avoid socialization and especially disclosure. However, most ministers readily empathize with burnout. Discussing your struggle honestly builds additional understanding. Secular individuals sometimes fail to understand your burnout, but they still need to understand your feelings and experiences. Healthy disclosure as discussed above builds friendship.

- *Inform* others about your burnout. Inform them that burnout and depression stimulate withdrawal that stimulates an ever-deepening destructive cycle of depression. Let them know that they fill a vital role in your recovery and ministry. You will feel surprised how many want to help. Since burnout and depression stimulate withdrawal, inform your friends that you might respond to them by withdrawing. Explain that the cycle results in a depletion of serotonin in the frontal cortex, so even when you know that socialization is necessary, you will probably find difficulty with accomplishing your intent to socialize.

- *Request* help from your friends. Give them permission to persist in their efforts to stimulate socialization. Ask them to schedule (in ink) a time of getting together every week. Schedule getting together with different friends at least three times every week.

Exercise 9-1: Construct your personal plan for promoting relationships. How will you incorporate the suggestions above into your personal plan?

CHAPTER 10

Emotional Resilience by Reversing Rumination

Wikipedia defines *rumination*, meaning "to chew the cud," as:

In animals, rumination is a part of normal digestion, in which the animal (known as a ruminant) brings up swallowed food (usually grass or hay), chews it, and swallows it. This aids the animal by allowing it to eat quickly and chew later while it is resting.

Humans may avoid coughing up their swallowed food to chew their cud, but some still ruminate. That is, when humans persistently and recurrently "chew the cud" by worrying about something, they ruminate, mentally.

When rumination occurs for only a short period of time, it helps us to identify new solutions to our problems. However, when we ruminate for weeks and months without end, the rumination spawns additional anxiety and a negative mood. Some individuals ruminate many hours every day. When Beth and I talk to a depressed minister about rumination, most respond that they ruminate habitually. Unfortunately, prolonged mental rumination causes depression.

Ministers ruminate over many things such as:

- Difficult relationships with friends and colleagues
- Marital problems
- The inability to keep nurturing a child who moved to another town after graduating from high school
- The lack of opportunity to mentor their wayward child
- A recent crisis event
- An upcoming transition such as moving to a different church or city, retirement, or a significant change in ministry
- A chronic medical illness
- A change in leadership

First of all, rumination seems normal, and in small doses, possibly even productive. We learn from our mistakes by ruminating a little over them and developing new solutions. After a short while, however, rumination serves no additional positive purpose. Then, it only magnifies our negative emotions, leads to apathy, results in withdrawal, and triggers the brain's circuits to respond with a chronic stress response including the reduction in serotonin production.

Reversing rumination requires forgiving others

Jesus clarifies the importance of forgiveness in Mark 11:25, "And when you stand praying, if you hold anything against anyone, forgive them, so that your Father in heaven may forgive you your sins." From what Jesus says, our forgiveness depends on forgiving others. We forgive "so that" our Father will forgive us. Christians ruminate over numerous things, but perhaps forgiveness acts as one of the more difficult ruminations to give up. Since Jesus told us to give up this type of rumination, we obviously can. Forgiving others requires reversing rumination about the injustice.

A highly experienced minister and leader found himself suddenly replaced by a much less experienced minister. He suffered from a great injustice that assaulted his core identity. And over the next eight years, we heard him ruminate and grieve over the injustice. Perhaps ministers ruminate more about injustices suffered from fellow ministers and staff members than any other source of suffering. Hardly any hurt feels as painful as the one received from someone within "your family." Reversing rumination requires letting go of personal injustices.

Worthington's (2005) REACH model includes five steps toward forgiveness. The plan replaces rumination associated with anger and unforgiveness with positive emotions.

1. Recall (R) the hurt. To heal, first recall the hurt as accurately as possible. Many individuals try to deny the hurt in an effort to eliminate their feelings. However, their feelings remain real.

2. Empathize (E). Try to see things from the other person's viewpoint. Empathy helps replace unforgiveness with understanding.

3. Act altruistic (A) by offering the gift of forgiveness. By acknowledging our own guilt over different offenses we can more easily value forgiveness. As we see ourselves needing forgiveness, we grow more willing to forgive others.

4. Commit (C) publicly to forgive. Committing publically helps the offended accept that he or she is truly forgiven.

5. Hold (H) onto forgiveness.

    •   The lingering pain from a hurt never represents unforgiveness. That is, the memory of the hurt including the pain may linger in spite of forgiveness.

    •   Replace rumination thoughts with deliberate thoughts of forgiveness.

    •   Keep reminding yourself that you have forgiven the other individual.

- Seek reassurance from friends and others.

Exercise 10-1: Construct your personal plan for promoting forgiveness. Who do you need to forgive? How will you incorporate the suggestions above into your personal plan?

Rumination—another word for worry

Scripture says something about rumination (worry). Jesus said, "Therefore I tell you, do not worry about your life, what you will eat or drink; or about your body, what you will wear. Is not life more important than food, and the body more important than clothes (Matthew 6:25). He went on to say, "Therefore do not worry about tomorrow, for tomorrow will worry about itself. Each day has enough trouble of its own (Matthew 6:34). The fact that Jesus tells us to stop worrying indicates that we can deliberately control our thoughts. Yet, most ministers privately acknowledge their struggle with habitual rumination.

Rumination—a lack of trust?

Psalm 57:1 says; "For in you my soul takes refuge; in the shadow of your wings I will take refuge until the destroying storms pass by." Thus, King David shows that reliance on the Lord ultimately eliminates the need for rumination. Instead, we can trust the Lord to provide justice. Perhaps trust in the Lord provides the first and most important step to reverse rumination.

Three skills give us the ability to break the rumination habit:

First, we can deliberately monitor our thoughts.

For example, program your cell phone alarm to go off every hour, and when it chimes, write down what you were thinking about when the alarm went off. Then, rate (between 0-10) your negative mood when the alarm rang. The following chart illustrates a rumination log:

Time	Activity	Rumination (minutes)	Negative Mood (0-10)
7:00	Got up from bed	5	1
8:00	Drove to work	15	7
9:00	Staff meeting	20	8
10:00	Meeting with a pastor	6	6
11:00	Developed sermon	9	9
12:00	Lunch	21	5
1:00	Back to work	12	4
2:00	Meeting	6	0
3:00	Developed course	24	8
4:00	Meeting	8	5
5:00	Drove home	25	9
6:00	Dinner	15	3
7:00	Helped children with homework	0	1
8:00	Talked to coworker	12	5
9:00	Watched TV	45	5
10:00	Got ready for bed	0	0
11:00	Slept	0	0
12:00	Slept	0	0
1:00	Awake for an hour	55	7
2:00	Slept	0	0

The Rumination Log provides a great source of information about what stimulates your rumination as well as the amount of your rumination. Many individuals report significant improvement after monitoring their hourly mood after as little as a week. Gradually, they learn to catch themselves as they first start to ruminate. As they ruminate, they can replace the negative thoughts with deliberate thoughts of trusting the Lord, trusting His ultimate justice, and trusting His control over our lives.

Exercise 10-2: Construct a rumination log, and program your watch or cell phone to go off every hour. Record your hourly thoughts. What did you learn about your rumination?

Second, we can monitor ourselves for high-risk environments.

The most prevalent high-risk environment generally occurs when we drift mentally, disengaged from any interesting mental activity. Daydreaming, watching TV, spending time alone, or engaging in repetitive (but boring) physical activities (such as driving on a freeway) stimulate rumination. Many ministers seem surprised that watching TV stimulates rumination. However, most TV shows are targeted at the sixth grade level. With so little mental stimulation required by the average TV show, most adults can easily predict the most likely ending to the story, and simultaneously ruminate about their problems.

Another high-risk environment occurs when we enter a discussion (or friendship) with someone who tends to ruminate. As both individuals ruminate together about some common negative event, both will leave feeling despondent. Sometimes, ministers form friendships around common negative events and people. These friendships seldom last longer than their common negative influence, but in the meantime both ministers feel progressively despondent. If you find yourself in such a relationship, please agree with your friend that you will discuss common negative influences for no more than ten minutes, at the most, during each of your times together. Otherwise, you may need to terminate this "toxic" friendship.

At times, ministers find that their quiet time with God is consumed with rumination and negativity. When this happens, focus on prayers of thanksgiving. Counting your blessings blocks rumination.

Many individuals report that they awaken at night unable to turn off their mind from negative thoughts. When this happens, focus on meditating on God's qualities and talking to Him. Somehow, talking to the Author of Peace generates a peaceful sleep.

Third, we can initiate an alternative activity that breaks the rumination cycle.

Scripture says, "Finally brothers, whatever is true, whatever is noble, whatever is right whatever is pure, whatever is lovely, whatever is admirable—if anything is excellent or praiseworthy—think about such things (Philippians 4:8). Instead of ruminating, we have innumerable choices of good things to consider. In chapter 11, you will identify things for which you feel thankful. However, we also challenge you to consider the following activities.

Mentally challenging activities, interpersonal conversation, or sports activities that require focused attention tend to break the rumination cycle. We recommend each minister identify activities in each of the following categories:

- Two mentally challenging activities (card games, educational courses, artistic endeavors).
- Three individuals (other than their spouse) with whom they can converse socially, at a moment's notice.
- Four sports activities (including exercise routines) that they enjoy and can pursue.

Many individuals find that sports activities break rumination. For instance, this I (Nathan) play table tennis almost every Sunday afternoon. As I focus to hit the ball, I cannot simultaneously ruminate about other events. Rumination causes me to miss the ball. Likewise, most competitive sports activities require focused attention at a level that makes rumination nearly impossible.

Likewise, authoring a sermon, a new course, or a journal article breaks rumination. Counseling others breaks rumination over one's own problems. For some individuals, listening to calming music breaks their rumination. Even playing a game of chess or a game of cards breaks rumination.

Rumination represents chronic negative thoughts. The best antidote to rumination comes from sitting in the presence of the God of Truth. Often we *talk* to God about our ruminations, trying to justify them. Negative thinking cannot persist when we sit and *listen* to the God of Truth.

Exercise 10-3: Construct your personal plan for eliminating rumination. How will you incorporate the suggestions above into your personal plan?

Listening to God offers the best reverse rumination activity possible.

CHAPTER 11

Emotional Resilience With Self-Esteem

As a nine-year-old missionary kid (MK), I (Nathan) remember itinerating in Arkansas with my parents. During itineration, my parents gave out hundreds of prayer cards. Each card included a small black-and-white photo of our family along with our names and the country to which we were going.

Like many MKs, I rejected Christianity in my early twenties and didn't come back to God until my early thirties. Finally, at fifty-two years of age, I became a missionary and was invited to participate in a missionary tour in Pennsylvania. When I arrived at a small country church, an elderly lady asked me, "Are you related to missionary Jim Davis from Arkansas?"

"Yes," I replied, "He is my father. Why do you ask?" From her purse, she pulled out a prayer card with our family photo. I was a nine-year-old child in the photo.

She explained that my father gave her the prayer card 43 years ago while he itinerated in Arkansas. Shortly afterward, her husband's employer transferred them to Pennsylvania, and she never knew what happened to our family. She concluded, "I came today to see if you were related to them. I wanted to let you know that I have been praying for you every day."

As I reflected on God's pursuit of me throughout my life, I learned a lesson, first-hand, about His persistence—God never stops pursuing His children. And, His disciples never stop loving each other, either. That old saint from Pennsylvania prayed for me for over forty years, never knowing what had happened to me. She proved that many unknown Christians love me almost as much as my heavenly Father does. She felt overjoyed to learn how God had answered her faithful prayers.

That day, my self-concept soared higher than ever before.

Exercise 11-1: Explain how God has intervened in your life to show how much He values you.

Self-Esteem—what develops it?

Self-esteem results from seeing a reflection (a mirror image) of ourselves as we interact with other individuals (Schiraldi, 1993, 17). It functions like looking into a mirror. When we see a reflection of ourselves through someone's reaction toward us, we use the information to determine our self-worth. Thus, self-esteem might be more appropriately called "other-esteem." It rarely comes from yourself, but it results from your perception of the other individual's opinion about you.

Exercise 11-2: Please explain how the following affects you:

If self-esteem results from our perception of another's opinion of us, what would be the expected normal effect on your self-esteem:

- If local individuals despise you as an *infidel* or as someone to avoid?
- If you work in an environment that seems ambivalent about

your ministry?

- If you work in a culture that devalues your wisdom and contribution to that society?
- If you feel isolated and find that you have few friends in your work location?
- If you suddenly perceive that local pastors, fellow missionaries, or even your leaders no longer value you?
- If your church lowers your salary?
- If others see you as easy prey to rob, pickpocket, hi-jack, kidnap, or exploit in any way possible?

Due to the above factors, no wonder that ambivalent and aggressive environments derail the minister's self-esteem. Self-esteem is damaged largely due to the negative image that one sees of himself or herself in the eyes of others. Chronic false beliefs reinforced by an ungodly culture fuel this negative self-image.

Fundamental Truth:

We lack self-esteem only because we believe a lot of things that are untrue! (Schiraldi, 1993)

What common false beliefs kill a minister's self-esteem?

Others should love and accept me. Ministers sometimes believe that others should welcome their skills into their sphere of influence and love them simply because they function as the hands of God. However, unless there is an extremely close personal relationship, this is probably an unrealistic expectation. In most cultures, no basis exists for others to love and accept us unless we have a close relationship. Since most North Americans fail to seek close relationships to the degree of those in other cultures, many fail to find love and acceptance through their relationships. If we, as Christians and ministers, experience difficulty loving and accepting our fellow co-workers, how realistic is it to expect that those who know us less will love and accept us more?

No one loves me. In contrast to the above belief, ministers sometimes believe that no one loves them. This, too, is false. No one knows the total sphere of influence that one develops over a lifetime of ministry. Thus, it seems unrealistic to assume that no one loves a minister simply because he or she is unable to see that love first-hand. Many Christians pray for a minister over a period of decades, even though they are known by little more than a thirty-minute sermon each week. Such dedication represents a Christ-like love. And, regardless of the love of others, God loves us enough that He called us into service with Him.

Others should recognize and value me. Ministers sometimes believe that others should automatically value them and their potential ministry. Although a minister may have received recognition and value in a previous church assignment, it is unrealistic to expect others in a new culture to recognize and value him or her in the same way. The minister may have accumulated a wealth of wisdom in one culture or location, but may receive little or no recognition of value in another.

I should always please others (live up to their expectations of me). Some ministers believe that they should always be able to please others. While working in a different culture, such a person endeavors to live up to the unspoken and unrealistic expectations of others. This type of individual is unable to adequately work through his or her personal issues because he or she is constantly trying to live up to the expectations of others. This attitude gives others control and leads to an unrealistically low self-esteem.

There is something wrong with me. Ministers almost always end up feeling that something is wrong with them. Usually, their error results from believing that something is wrong with them, personally, instead of realizing that a failed relationship, or an illness, or some other contingency might have prompted their disappointment. Regardless, almost all ministers eventually feel that something is wrong with them simply because they experience emotional numbness, guild, loss of appetite, sleep, concentration, and energy during times of stress and trauma. These uncomfortable feelings are not normal for them. However, the belief that something is wrong with them is a misperception. It is normal to have negative feelings during any stress or trauma, and especially in an aggressive environment. These emotions and symptoms are a normal reaction to an ungodly environment. These are normal feelings for a very abnormal event and a very abnormal environment. The event, not the feeling, is abnormal.

I am defective and inferior to other people. Almost all ministers feel inferior to those who have spectacular results. Each minister, however, possesses many skills that have been honed over decades of ministry. The challenge is to find new ways to use those skills instead of lingering in feelings of inferiority. God values each individual equally, including the one who may be handicapped in some way, including a cross-cultural awkwardness. All are valued, equally. There is no inferior minister. He or she has "run the good race, and fought the good fight." The Apostle Paul was able to exclaim, "I have kept the faith, I have finished the course." As a joint heir with Christ, you are an *overcomer*.

I am hopeless—there is no future ministry for me. Ministry can easily leave one feeling defeated. The number and gravity seem impossible for us to solve by ourselves, but they are never too big for God. He gives us countless friends with whom we can interact for additional insights. With Christ at our helm, hope abounds. Even when we totally fail in the assignment to which we were called, there is a future, especially in ministry. "These three remain: faith, hope, and love."

I should always feel respected and viewed as perfect. Ministers are often put on a super-spiritual pedestal of near-sainthood by individuals in their local church. When exalted to near-sainthood long enough, it is easy for them to start believing the expectations of the local church members. Subsequently, as they start to feel anger and resentment during times of stress and victimization, they naturally feel guilt, stemming from the belief that one ***should*** be perfect. They fail to accept that they are merely human, not yet perfectly sanctified. The truth is that while everyone likes perfection, we are all merely growing spiritually. No minister is perfect this side of heaven.

I am unworthy. Many Christians, including ministers, sometimes believe that they are unworthy. The truth is that we all **WERE** unworthy, filthy, and wretched. However, we are now joint-heirs with Christ. We are no longer unworthy and filthy any more than our joint-heir, Jesus Himself. We are now spotless, redeemed, and made worthy through the blood of the Lamb.

Exercise 11-3: Explain which of the above beliefs plagued you in the past, or still provide a problem now.

Exercise 11-4: The following laws were adapted and edited for style from Howard's Laws as described in Building Self-Esteem, A 125 Day Program (Schiraldi, 1993, 25). Using your Bible and concordance, please search for at least two Scripture verses that substantiate the following laws of our unconditional worth before God:

God values you infinitely and eternally.

Scripture #1:

Scripture # 2:

How has God shown you that He values you infinitely and eternally?

God values each individual equally. Therefore, the following externals neither add to nor diminish from our worth:

- Our market worth (how much money we can earn)
- Our social worth (how many friends esteem us)
- Our ability to perform or accomplish tasks

Scripture #1:

Scripture # 2:

How has God shown you that He values each individual equally?

Your worth is complete in Christ, but it is not completed.

Scripture #1:

Scripture # 2:

How has God shown you that your worth is complete in Christ, but not completed?

God's assessment of your eternal value never changes (even if someone rejects you, or when—not *if*—you fail).

Scripture #1:

Scripture #2:

How has God shown you that His assessment of your eternal value never changes?

God never stops pursuing you and your children.

Scripture #1:

Scripture # 2:

How has God shown you that He never stops pursuing you or your children?

Exercise 11-5: If self-esteem comes from seeing a reflection of ourselves as we look at others, describe the kind of self-esteem that is possible when we look toward other Christians, including our mission leaders, other pastors, and other individuals?

Exercise 11-6: If self-esteem comes from seeing a reflection of ourselves as we look at others, describe the kind of self-esteem that results if we fail to look toward God, i.e., fail to have daily devotional time with Him? What is your plan for devotions?

Fundamental Truths:

- We lack self-esteem only because we believe a lot of things that are untrue (Schiraldi, 1993).

- We cannot value our self if we do not spend time with the One (God) who values us in truth!

- "You are all sons of God through faith in Christ Jesus, for all of you who were baptized into Christ have clothed yourselves with Christ. There is neither Jew nor Greek, slave nor free, male nor female, for you are all one in Christ Jesus. If you belong to Christ, then you are Abraham's seed, and heirs according to the promise (Galatians 3:26-29)."

- "So you are no longer a slave, but a son; and since you are a son, God has made you also an heir (Galatians 4:7)."

Exercise 11-7: Evaluate how the above four truths apply to you as a minister. Describe how these truths apply to your personal self-esteem.

CHAPTER 12

Emotional Resilience With Personal Goals

For over 100 years a few small agricultural villages in Pennsylvania, Ohio, and Indiana have thrived with personal contentment and simplicity. The residents reject electricity, modern conveniences, and still use horses and mules to till the ground. Women who show a personal interest in knitting, cross stitching, quilting, sewing, or cooking frequently pursue their interests, almost always with the blessing of others. Men who show a personal interest in trapping, gardening, construction, or woodwork also pursue their interests. Men socialize frequently with other men as they barter at the local cattle auction. Meanwhile, women gather to sew and knit, while catching up on the neighborhood gossip. The agricultural lifestyle provides plenty of hard work with the added benefit of outdoor exercise.

These communities frown on divorce and highly value fidelity in marriage. Children tend to settle down near the village when they mature, and family interaction continues as a strong value lasting over multiple generations. Each individual fills a role in the village that provides a meaningful purpose to others—they live interdependently. The village and families esteem the elderly for their wisdom. Nursing homes are unnecessary—each family cares for the extended family. For the most part, villagers attend worship together. Other than times of planting and harvest, many individuals use their spare time in the winter months to develop new skills associated with their work and trade. And despite their difficult lifestyle, the village inhabitants very rarely witness burnout or depression (Egeland and Hostetter, 1990). Just like 100 years ago, these villages continue today as Amish communities.

Rather than moving to an Amish community, we encourage you to learn from their burnout-resistant lifestyle.

Exercise 12-1: How does the culture described above differ from yours as related to the following factors:

1. Ability to pursue personal goals.
2. Ability to pursue times of leisure.
3. Ability to spend time together as a family.
4. Ability to maintain and pursue health and fitness.
5. Ability to pursue friendships.
6. Ability to pursue intimacy with a significant other.
7. Ability to pursue spiritual goals.
8. Ability to pursue academic goals.

Exercise 12-2: If a lifestyle similar to the Amish lifestyle ever existed previously in your culture, what caused it to change?

Peterson. (2006, 92) reports the following correlations between life conditions and life satisfaction.

0 to Small Correlation	Moderate Correlation	Large Correlation
Age	Number of friends	Gratitude
Gender	Being married	Optimism

Education	Religiousness	Being employed
Social class	Level of leisure activity	Frequency of sexual intercourse
Income	Physical health	% of time with positive affect
Having children	Conscientiousness	Happiness of identical twins
Ethnicity	Extraversion	Self-esteem
Intelligence	Neuroticism (a negative correlation)	
Physical attractiveness	Internal locus of control	

Reflecting on the correlations in the Moderate and Large Correlation columns above, many of the factors correlated to happiness and life satisfaction represent individual choices for relationships. That is, factors in the right two columns represent conditions about which you exercise some degree of control. Unfortunately, the Christian culture in many countries (especially North America) fails to value these choices as much as the choices in the "0 to small" column.

Other factors that bring life satisfaction include physical health, leisure activity, religiousness (spiritual goals), being married (intimacy), and internal locus of control. Internal locus of control includes the ability to pursue personal goals as well as the ability to engage in goal planning. To a large degree, Peterson's study largely substantiates the contented Amish lifestyle and the eight areas listed above.

Exercise 12-3: In what ways have ministers in your present culture syncretized their lifestyle to pursue modern industrialized values more than the eight areas listed?

The importance of goals

Robert Emmons (1999, 15) states, "Human beings are by nature goal oriented," and their "behavior is organized around the pursuit of goals." Emmons notes that one's goals "are potent contributors to their overall levels of happiness."

In the *Handbook of Hope* (1994), C. R. Snyder shows that hopeful thinking doesn't happen automatically—it requires intentional thought and planning. While pre-industrialized societies inherently promoted the above eight factors that increase hopeful thinking, individuals in modern cultures must intentionally engage in goal planning across these domains to increase hopeful thinking.

Consider for a moment: Without goals across all of life's domains, pastors and missionaries often feel hopeless when their church—or denominational leader—suddenly asks them to leave or when they find their work goals blocked. That is, when a work-related goal provides the minister with his or her sole meaningful goal, anything blocking that single goal tends to devastate the minister's hope and self-worth. Sir Francis Bacon said, "A wise man will make more opportunities than he finds." Indeed, a wise minister will make a variety of goals for almost all areas of his or her life.

Intentional planning builds hope

In the *Handbook of Hope* (Ibid.), Snyder shows that hopeful thinking grows as an individual builds goals across each of nine broad domains of life (the eight domains listed above plus the work domain). If you build meaningful goals in each domain, you can retain a positive hopeful outlook even when (not if) some event firmly blocks one of those goals.

For instance, language school commonly blocks missionary goals toward a meaningful ministry for a year or so. Missionaries report frustration and even some degree of depression during the time that language study blocks their direct pursuit of ministry. However, those with goals across the remaining domains seem to persist much better.

Similarly, those who must leave one church to transition to another commonly report frustration with the amount of time and effort required to set up a new house and ministry. Their ministry goals remain firmly blocked by the logistics of the move and the grief of leaving their previous assignment. Those with clear goals across the remaining domains of life, however, seem resistant to burnout during their transition. They still retain a meaningful life by pursuing meaningful goals in all the remaining domains of life.

We invite you to design your goals using the acrostic: SMART. SMART goals are Specific, Measurable, Attainable, Realistic, and Time-lined. Please see the YouTube playlist referenced on page 31, and select the video titled "Setting SMART Objectives" to help you with this process. In the Handbook of Hope (Ibid.), Snyder shows that a resilient and hopeful individual forms goals not only for their job and occupation, but more importantly across the following eight domains of life:

Personal growth goals

A young missionary child enjoyed working with computers and writing computer programs. He also felt called into missions. After finishing Bible College, he applied for missionary appointment and moved to minister in a foreign country. Never feeling totally content without computers nearby, he continued pursuing additional computer courses. As his computer skills and education matured, he grew more and more able to help others with their computer problems. Eventually, his denominational leadership asked him to transition and supervise the computer department at their headquarters. Many bystanders had believed that his interest in computers represented a waste of time.

An alarmingly large percentage of ministers tend to focus on ministry goals exclusively, and neglect personal growth. That is, they pursue ministry related goals exclusively but never develop their personal interests. When we fail to develop inherent areas of interest, we may unwittingly thwart areas of future ministry. God frequently works "out-of-the-box," using these unique and novel interests in ways that we never foresee.

Exercise 12-4:

- With what interests outside of ministry has God gifted you?
- What are your goals for developing these interests? What SMART goals will help you pursue each of these interests?

Leisure goals

When ministers have few leisure goals, it is often because they carry multiple ministerial responsibilities. Sometimes they even act as if leisure represents an immoral activity.

One minister lamented that he never took a day off. He needed a break, but he felt stuck in a culture that ruled out vacations and leisure. The local parishioners and other ministers ridiculed him if he considered taking a vacation. He felt doomed if he did, and doomed if he didn't.

How do you feel about breaking one of the Ten Commandments?

The commandment regarding the Sabbath Day is the longest and most detailed. The Bible says, "Remember the Sabbath day by keeping it holy. Six days you shall labor and do all your work, but the seventh day is a Sabbath to the LORD your God. On it you shall not do any work, neither you, nor your son or daughter, nor your manservant or maidservant, nor your animals, nor the alien within your gates. For in six days the LORD made the heavens and the earth, the sea, and all that is in them, but he rested on the seventh day. Therefore the LORD blessed the Sabbath day and made it holy (Ex 20:8-11, NIV)."

A few ministers take this commandment literally. They work long hours for six days of the week, and then rest on the Sabbath. While this commandment fails to address every detail of implementation, the intent is fairly clear—model God's behavior by taking a periodic rest.

Was God so worn out that He needed to rest on the Sabbath? I doubt that He ever grows physically tired. If God doesn't need physical rest, what prompted Him to explain this commandment in such minute detail? Two possibilities come to mind:

First, God wanted to model healthy behaviors to His followers. The commandment explicitly notes how God models the rhythm of work and rest, "For in six days the LORD made the heavens and the earth, the sea, and all that is in them, but he rested on the seventh day." By noting that God rested after six days of work, the commandment implies that He wishes for humankind to follow His behavior. A corollary implication is that God avoided modeling burnout and wishes for His creation to do the same.

A friend recently told me, "If I die early from burnout, I simply get to spend one extra day with the Lord." If we follow a different pattern than what God designed, we choose an imperfect model. Although the commandment never uses the word "burnout," the commandment specifically encourages rest. Thus behaviors resulting in burnout are ungodly.

Second, the consequence of rest affects so much that God wanted the commandment to include everything within our power and control—sons, daughters, menservants, maidservants, animals, and even the alien on our property. In today's environment, most of us don't own farm animals, but we have power and control over many individuals and objects. We can, however, affect our congregation's expectations about Sabbath rest and the expectations of our colleagues. God gives us much power and control if we choose to exercise it. Reflect for a moment about your span of power and control.

What happens during Sabbath?

For humankind, the commandment states that everything we control should rest during Sabbath. However, we don't control much in comparison to God. He remains in control even as we rest.

Although we can't know everything He accomplishes during this time, when we rise the next morning we can easily see that He has continued working. During our Sabbath, God continues to prepare His creation for our interface. For humankind, however, Sabbath means a time of rest. God commands us to rest and to cause everything within our control to rest.

When does Sabbath start?

Although "the Sabbath Day" occurs once every seven days, Sabbath occurs each night when we fall asleep. For instance, Adam and Eve probably went to bed at dusk and awakened at dawn each day. Without the electrical lights of a modern culture, they fell into a normal rhythm of rest (Sabbath) about eight to ten hours each day.

Today, technology enables us to literally "burn the candle at both ends," working late into the night and rising to start work well before dawn. If God wants us to put aside one full day each week for rest, failure to rest adequately during the intervening nights may also violate the intent of His commandment.

Just like Adam and Eve, God made us in His image. God designed an environment that almost forced Adam and Eve to sleep eight or more hours each night. Because of electricity, we can now choose a significantly different model of rest than the one He provided. While electricity is wonderful, we can use it in a harmful way.

Thus Sabbath means rest during one day, but the intent of the law may also include the natural rhythms of rest throughout the week. If God promotes rest on a Sabbath, it makes little sense to promote a burnout lifestyle during the intervening days.

What does the Bible say about rhythms?

Matthew 11:28-30 (The Message) says, "Are you tired? Worn Out? Burned out on religion? Come to me. Get away with me and you'll recover your life. I'll show you how to take a real rest. Walk with me and work with me—watch how I do it. Learn the unforced rhythms of grace. I won't lay anything heavy or ill-fitting on you. Keep company with me and you'll learn to live freely and lightly."

This passage references God's numerous "rhythms of grace." A Sabbath Day rest provides one primary rhythm. Other rhythms include a nightly rest, daily work, socialization, meals, Scripture reading, and prayer; fasting; community with fellow believers; and many more. In this particular passage, Jesus mentions a "rhythm" of rest. Just as the Genesis passage requires us to model our rest and work cycle after God, the Matthew passage reminds us to look toward God (Jesus) as our model.

How does my life compare to His?

We can look at many New Testament passages to see how Jesus modeled the rhythm of rest. For instance,

He went up on a mountain side and sat down.

He walked beside the Sea of Galilee.

He got into the boat.

He had dinner at Matthew's house.

He went out and sat by the lake.

He left the crowd and went into the house.

He withdrew by boat privately to a solitary place.

…and when evening came, he reclined at the table with his friends.

Early in the morning, Jesus stood on the shore.

Jesus took with Him, Peter, James, and John.

Thus, we can see that Jesus modeled many rhythms including the rhythms of work and rest. And, He modeled rest at many times other than the Sabbath Day.

How does my life compare to the early church fathers?

Richard Foster (27) states that the early church fathers valued *Otium Sanctum* (holy leisure). They believed that all activities of the day remained holy, including leisure time. To them, leisure was inherently holy. This included spiritual activities of the soul such as retreat, restoration, and play. For them, the spiritual life integrated (rather than isolated) holy leisure into the daily life of the believer.

May God offer you inspiration as you seek His help in modeling His rhythm of work and rest.

Exercise 12-5:

- What leisure activities would you like to pursue (gardening, camping, fishing, hiking, photography, photo editing, reading, cooking, music lessons, listening to your favorite music)?
- What SMART goals will help you pursue each of these interests?

Family goals

Humans adapt rapidly to the luxuries they buy. The adaptation happens so rapidly that any happiness from their purchase seems relatively short-lived compared to things that produce a lasting happiness. North Americans, in particular, tend to discount things that produce lasting happiness, such as social relationships with friends and family. Instead many tend to buy toys and luxuries that fail to produce a lasting happiness.

Economist Robert Frank found that people pursue activities and purchase many things that don't make economic sense. He concludes, "People would be happier and healthier if they took more time off and 'spent' it with their family and friends, yet North Americans have long headed in the opposite direction." In what ways do ministers in your culture pursue activities in preference to family goals? What specific family goals seem meaningful to pursue?

Many ministers feel unable to pursue family-oriented goals due to physical separation from their relatives. However, modern technology enables telephone with video over the Internet and many other ways to connect with family.

How can you help guide the next generation in your family? Consider your potentially changing role toward family members, e.g., you may change from doing active work to advising. Consider any need to help aging parents, ailing spouses, or needy grandchildren. Consider if you need to visit your family more frequently to accomplish your family goals. How can you balance your need to remain independent (not enmeshed) in the lives of parents and children who are becoming less able to care for themselves, even while offering care to those same individuals?

Exercise 12-6: My family SMART goals are:

- My spouse –
- My children –
- My brothers/sisters–
- My parents –
- Others –

Health and fitness goals

Hopefully, some of your health and fitness goals changed while digesting Chapter 5. What are your goals for pursuing health and fitness? Physical activity increases a positive outlook and helps maintain mental sharpness (Hill, Storandt, & Malley, 1993).

Exercise 12-7: Since a significant portion of your life still remains, how will you ensure that your health and fitness enables the fullest possible lifestyle? Complete the following plan:

- I will maintain good sleep patterns of...
- I will eat a healthy, balanced diet such as…
- I will avoid foods such as …
- My plan to maintain a healthy body weight is ….
- My plan for daily exercise is…
- Medication—I will take the following medication and supplements:

Friendship goals

Hopefully, some of your health and fitness goals changed while reading Chapter 9. What are your goals for developing and strengthening friendships? Due to the constant mobility and uncertainness of their ministry, few ministers retain close relationships. They build a multitude of casual friendships among colleagues but few intimate friendships.

Researchers Leaf Van Boven and Tom Gilovich (2003) investigated two groups of subjects, one that spent money on a material possession and the other on an experience or activity. Those who spent money on an experience such as a ski trip, concert, or a great meal were happier and believed that that their money was better spent than those who described buying a material object such as clothing, jewelry, or electronics. However, they also found that those who spent money on activities almost always spent the money on activities with other individuals. Experiences give happiness because they increase social connection. Thus, money spent on activities often connects us to others and brings happiness while money spent on objects tends to separate us.

We witnessed an example of this truth when we ministered in the Philippines. A Pilipino might struggle to make a living but derive great pleasure from throwing parties and dinner celebrations for his friends and extended family. In contrast, business executives from highly industrialized countries invest their income on elaborate homes, sport cars, boats, and high-tech gadgets. Although Pilipinos often receive ridicule from their international counterparts, their close relationships bring more happiness than money spent on material objects.

Referring back to the Peterson (2006) life satisfaction correlations on page 115 of this chapter, many of the factors in his "moderate and large" columns relate to bringing people together: number of friends, being married, religiousness, extraversion, being employed, sexual intercourse, and self-esteem. Thus, a "happy hermit" represents an oxymoron.

In many countries, people actively pursue friendship. As a child growing up in Japan, I (Nathan) learned this value from my Japanese friend, Saito. Because of his choice to accept Jesus, Saito's family and friends rejected him, and his employer fired him. Saito's parents, brothers and sisters no longer acknowledged he even existed. So, during my last year of high school, Saito and I grew close. We played baseball and volleyball together almost every weekend. Saito never called me "Nathan." Saito called me "Brother Nathan" and put more meaning into the word "brother" than anyone else.

Eventually, however, I graduated from high school and returned to the States. Several years later, I decided to get married. Few of my family members and certainly none of my friends from Japan could travel over 6,000 miles to attend my Stateside wedding. So I knew that the bride's side of the church would fill with guests, while the groom's side would remain nearly empty. In a Japanese culture, such a predicament meant that I would "lose face." More importantly, I needed to keep my friends from "losing face." Knowing their expense and difficulty in attending, I delayed mailing the wedding invitations to give them a good excuse with which they could save face for not attending. Three weeks before the wedding, I finally dropped the invitations in the mail.

The wedding ceremony started almost as I expected. At the appointed cue, I walked briskly to the front of the sanctuary, turned toward the audience, and strained to see anyone I knew in the audience. My father stood at the podium, my mother sat with my aunt Polly on the front pew on the groom's side. And that was all—the groom's side looked nearly empty. Even worse, the bride's side almost overflowed! In the North American culture, this predicament looked minor, but coming from my Japanese culture, I felt humiliated.

Then, just before the service started, Saito walked in. Not knowing about the American wedding custom of letting the usher seat each guest, Saito ignored the ushers and proceeded down the aisle to find his own seat. He walked all the way to the front. Upon arriving at my mother's pew, Saito turned and smiled at me. As Saito and I stood there looking at each other, I remembered Jesus' words, "Who is My mother and who are My brothers?" And stretching out His hand toward His disciples, Jesus said, "Behold, My mother and My brothers!" (Matt. 12:47-49).

Saito sat down beside my mother. As he sat down, I heard several not-so-silent gasps at the sight of a short foreigner sitting with the groom's family. Nevertheless, Saito, in his naiveté, knew his correct place. My *brother* had arrived, and regardless of anyone else's absence or presence, I knew that the groom's side was now complete. The ceremony began.

Following the reception, I asked Saito how he obtained an immigration visa on such a short notice. He replied, "I simply handed the wedding invitation to the government official and said, "This is my brother."

Exercise 12-8: Describe your SMART goals (and plan) to develop meaningful relationships in your ministry location.

Intimacy goals

Jonathan Haidt states (2006, 140), "The reality that people often wake up to is that life is a gift they have been taking for granted, and that people matter more than money." Most ministers value people more than money or they would never enter the ministry. However, some ministers value ministry more than people. In your pursuit of ministry, do you overlook developing and maintaining intimacy with your spouse and close friends?

Exercise 12-9:

- If people really matter to you, what are your SMART goals to develop intimacy with your spouse and closest friends?
- To whom will you talk about your deepest troubles and

feelings?

- Please note that intimacy may include those outside of your spousal relationship. Often it includes one or two close friends. Unmarried ministers often overlook their need for intimacy, even with close friends.

Spiritual goals

What are your spiritual goals? Note that ministry goals remain distinctly different than spiritual goals. Spiritual goals deepen your personal relationship with God. Emmons (1999, 108) notes that spiritual strivings have an "empowering function" that "can confer coherence upon the personality." That is, spiritual strivings integrate all of one's other strivings "in the face of constant environmental and cultural pressures that push for fragmentation." Thus spiritual strivings, more than any other strivings, act to integrate and stabilize the minister going through transition. "The hallmark of the psychologically healthy person is integration" (Ibid., 118).

Exercise 12-10:

- What account do you hope to give for your spiritual life? Is the life that you live the one that you wanted to live?
- What SMART spiritual goals will you carry into your next phase of life?
- At what time of the day will you maintain daily devotions?
- How long will you spend daily in prayer?
- How long will you spend in daily Bible study? How long will you journal the insights that God provides?
- With whom and how will you connect to reflect about what God is revealing to you?

Academic goals

Peterson (2006, 92) reports many correlations between life

conditions and life satisfaction (see page 115). His study shows that education fails to correlate with life satisfaction. However, the effect of past educational accomplishments remains quite different than the effect of present and future academic pursuits. Snider (1994) shows that academic pursuit builds an internal locus of self-control (a sense of self-efficacy). Self-efficacy builds hopeful thinking and self-esteem. And hopeful thinking and self-esteem build resilience.

When I (Nathan) planned to retire from working for the Air Force, I spent four years taking new educational courses, all prior to transitioning into ministry. What initially stimulated high anxiety resulted in progressively lower anxiety as I prepared fully for a new ministry and a new lifestyle. The success of the transition depended on four years of detailed plans and education. As you plan for continued ministry, what new academic goals are needed to support your development?

Dr. Joseph Castleberry, president of Northwest University, also served as a missionary to Ecuador. He makes the following observation about possibilities for life-long learning:

> No matter what age or phase of ministry a particular student may be in, seminary and formal education can play a crucial role in providing them with tools that will take them to a new level of professionalism. Just as important, seminary study occurs in the context of deep commitment to the presence and anointing of the Holy Spirit, whom Jesus desires to pour out on the young and the old, on men and women, and on people of diverse racial and ethnic backgrounds and walks of life.

Exercise 12-11:

- What are your academic goals? Lifelong learning represents a fundamental element of well-being. What courses would help you better accomplish your call and your personal growth?
- What SMART academic goals will you pursue?

CHAPTER 13

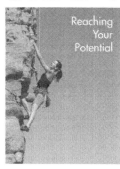

Reaching Your Potential

Emotional Resilience With Ministry Goals

When C. S. Lewis (1970) was asked which religion provides the greatest happiness, he replied "While it lasts, the religion of worshipping oneself is the best" (p 33). He went on to state that he didn't use religion to make himself happy. He said that a bottle of port wine would do that.

There is more to life than seeking happiness.

Those in ministry well know that their work often includes suffering and rejection. Sometimes they expect their call to automatically produce happiness. However, responding to the "call" isn't about happiness so much as providing a *choice* to flourish in joy.

The "call" provides a pathway toward joy

The "call" provides each minister with a choice to flourish in joy or wither in something less. Most ministers recognize that their call will lead to joy rather than happiness. Joy results from a meaningful life and specifically from following God's "call." C. S Lewis noted that a great difference exists between a meaningful life (with joy) and a happy life. Thus, happiness seems related to joy, but joy may or may not include happiness.

Regardless, recent research into happiness provides a few clues that apply to those who seek joy as well as happiness. After years of research, Lyubomirsky, Sheldon, Schkade, and Seligman (2008) found the following "happiness formula:"

$$H = S + C + V$$

Where:

H represents the level of happiness,

S represents your biological set point,

C represents the conditions of your life, and

V represents voluntary activities that you perform.

When correctly applied to the minister's call, this formula provides a pathway that affects meaningfulness and joy. Since the biological set-point (S) is determined genetically, efforts to change one's set-point seem futile. However, ministers possess greater control over C and V than almost any other people group in the world. If the happiness formula rings true, minister have a higher potential for happiness than anyone else in the world. So why are a few ministers. so unhappy with their call, and worse yet, devoid of joy?

Buddhism, Hinduism, and Stoicism teach that happiness occurs only by looking within oneself. Thus, these religions teach that C and V remain irrelevant to happiness. That is, they teach that happiness results from suppressing your feelings about the conditions of life (i.e., developing numbness to the conditions of life). Additionally, they teach that your state of mind is more important than the outward activities (V) that you might perform. However, research shows that many conditions (C) in life such as the lack of control, shame, and the quality of relationships significantly affect happiness. And the activities of your life (V) also significantly affect happiness. So the research evidence on happiness shows that Buddhism, Hinduism, and Stoicism have it all wrong—their formula may produce peaceful feelings, but peacefulness remains quite different than happiness or joy. Smoking marijuana, numbness and death all provide some measure of peace. Many psychologists readily point out that numbness and the peace that results from numbness represent key symptoms of depression. So peace isn't too satisfying, after all. I have heard a few Miss Universe contestants state that they want world peace, but when sought at the cost of drugs, numbness and death, peace fails to satisfy. In contrast to a call to numbness and escape, ministers respond to a call to action (V).

V (voluntary activities) provides a pathway toward happiness and joy

V (the minister's call to voluntary service) significantly affects happiness and more importantly, joy. Haidt (2006) reports some interesting research on V (voluntary activities). He asked 350 subjects to engage in four activities over several days. In one activity, the subjects indulged their senses by eating ice cream in the middle of each day. In a second activity, they attended a lecture that they normally might avoid. In a third activity, they performed an act of kindness for a friend who needed cheering up. In a fourth activity, they recorded a reason for feeling gratitude toward someone, and then telephoned them to express their gratitude. Haidt found that people experienced longer-lasting improvements in mood from acts of kindness and gratitude than acts in which they indulged themselves. Thus, V causes a real improvement in happiness. Happiness isn't about finding a way to feel detached from the world by numbing oneself. And it isn't about indulging oneself in ice cream, alcohol, or other drugs. By voluntarily using their strengths, especially in service to others, ministers around the world increase happiness in themselves as well as their neighbors.

A well-known Hungarian researcher, Csikszentmihalyi (pronounced "cheeks sent me high"), found that humans worldwide value a type of V called "flow" more highly than even sex. Many ministers seem characterized by "flow." Haidt (2006) calls flow, "A state of total immersion in a task that is challenging yet closely matched to one's abilities." For ministers, nothing represents "flow" more than following their "call" to engage in a task that is always extraordinary challenging. Although the tasks *always* remain beyond their abilities, God *always* bestows His ability perfectly matched to the call. And therefore most "called" ministers quickly succumb to total immersion in the call. For the minister with flow, he or she sees a clear challenge that fully engages their attention, they have the ability (with God's enablement) to accomplish the call, and they often receive feedback (from the Spirit and others) on how they are doing at each step of their call. With the inspiration of the Spirit, the called minister has an inside track to developing the strongest "flow" possible. These individuals have the highest internal motivation conceivable.

Seligman notes that the key to finding your flow is to know your strengths. Avoiding your weaknesses or delegating those activities to someone else remains equally important. As an example, a reliable personality inventory shows that a friend of mine loves science, exploration, and new and novel ideas. In contrast, he intensely dislikes mundane or repetitious activities and "in-the-box" ways of thinking. To apply personality strengths toward his call, he tries to find new and novel ways to translate research (and other forms of science) into practical tools for others. While reading through research reports that others consider dry and mundane, he feels excitement and awe as he discovers new ways to apply research to help others. Since he dislikes mundane and "in-the-box" ways of thinking, he naturally dislikes administrative tasks. He quickly notes the discrepancy between his personality and the personality of an administrative specialist such as an accountant. In contrast to him, accountants that implement new and novel ways of thinking usually end up in jail. So he happily delegates his weakness related tasks to others. Thus, his life is characterized by pursuit of his strengths while avoiding his weaknesses.

Ministers perhaps have the greatest freedom to pursue a call that maximizes their strengths while avoiding their weaknesses. Most can readily identify and enthusiastically pursue their call. However, a few others struggle at identifying strengths and weaknesses.

Exercise 13-1: What are your strengths and weaknesses?

To help you evaluate the types of ministry activities that you might enjoy or want to avoid, please rate the following thirty-one job characteristics on the scale shown at the left of each item. These characteristics are taken from a body of research on personality measurement. Please rate how much you like or dislike these job characteristics. However, do NOT rate your present job—instead rate what you would inherently like or dislike in any job. Circle a number anywhere between 1-5, 1=you very much dislike the characteristic, 2=you somewhat dislike the characteristic, 3=you neither like nor dislike the characteristic, 4=you somewhat like the characteristic, 5=you very much like the characteristic.

Note that no specific scoring method exists for this exercise. However, completing the inventory will give you a starting-point for thinking about your personal enjoyment or distaste for certain kinds of work.

Item #	Rating	Description or Characteristic
1	1 2 3 4 5	Social interaction is required by the job.
2	1 2 3 4 5	Marketing skills are required by the job.
3	1 2 3 4 5	Personal recognition is provided through the job.
4	1 2 3 4 5	Public speaking is required by the job.
5	1 2 3 4 5	Reclusiveness is enabled by the job.

6	1 2 3 4 5	Autonomy (control my own work assignment) is provided by the job.
7	1 2 3 4 5	Assertiveness is required by the job.
8	1 2 3 4 5	Leadership is required by the job.
9	1 2 3 4 5	Creativity is required by the job.
10	1 2 3 4 5	Cognitive activity and problem solving are required.
11	1 2 3 4 5	Artistic expression is required by the job.
12	1 2 3 4 5	Scientific orientation is required by the job.
13	1 2 3 4 5	Hard physical labor is required by the job.
14	1 2 3 4 5	Reflective/philosophical thinking is required by the job.
15	1 2 3 4 5	Supervision from others is required by the job.
16	1 2 3 4 5	Ambiguity in my work functions is inherent in the job.
17	1 2 3 4 5	Warmth and sympathy are required by the job.
18	1 2 3 4 5	Sympathy is required by the job.
19	1 2 3 4 5	Gentleness is required by the job.
20	1 2 3 4 5	Friendliness is required by the job.
21	1 2 3 4 5	Helpfulness is required by the job.
22	1 2 3 4 5	Acceptance—I feel accepted in this job.
23	1 2 3 4 5	Inflexible deadlines are required by the job.
24	1 2 3 4 5	Conflict is an inherent part of the job.
25	1 2 3 4 5	Feelings of powerlessness are inherent in the job.
26	1 2 3 4 5	Organization and attention to small details are required.
27	1 2 3 4 5	Unending responsibilities (24 hrs./day) are required by the job.
28	1 2 3 4 5	Persistence is required by the job.
29	1 2 3 4 5	Control of others is required by the job.

30	1 2 3 4 5	My integrity is inherently questioned in the job.
31	1 2 3 4 5	Stress is inherent in the job.

Reflecting on your ratings above, list the characteristics that represent your strengths:

Reflecting on your ratings above, what made your previous ministry activities enjoyable (power, control, leadership, autonomy, clear direction, creativity, team relationships, meaningfulness, service, feedback, recognition, acceptance, etc.)? Ask for help from your spouse or friends to develop a complete list of previous ministry activities that you enjoyed along with the reasons why you enjoyed them.

Ministry Activities   Reasons for Enjoyment

Write a true story about an event that brought out the best in you. After reflecting on it, what did you learn about yourself from this event?

Reflecting on your ratings above, list your weaknesses:

Reflecting on your ratings in the above inventory, what ministry roles and job functions do you dislike and want to avoid?

Ministry Activities   Reasons for Displeasure

Other than the ministry roles and job functions listed above, what additional ministry roles and functions take advantage of the type of activities that you enjoy? How can you use your strengths in novel ways?

What types of ministries would you like to do that you never got around to doing?

Exercise 13-2: During your ministry, what kinds of activities have you accomplished well even though you disliked them? Most ministers, through necessity, develop skills for activities that they dislike. Reminisce for a moment about those activities and events. This list will include functions and ministries in which you need to protect yourself from getting re-engaged. For instance during a summer break in high school, I worked on a crew building houses. Since I am not called into missions to construct buildings, I know that I need to take special precautions against getting involved in building projects. What kinds of activities have you accomplished well but need to avoid in your call?

Exercise 13-3: Has God called you to perform specific unmistakable tasks? Note that God called the prophet Jonah to perform specific tasks that he disliked. Your ministry may require activities that you dislike, too. Please note that for some individuals, finding their niche of ministry is often more about them than about God. So, we invite you to consider that His plan may consider other factors that remain more important than your particular likes and dislikes. Has God called you to do something specifically? Has He put you in a place that you can contribute something to His kingdom that is outside of your comfort zone? Please list these specific callings.

Exercise 13-4: To refocus your calling, please try the following exercise from Peterson (2006, 3): think a moment about the very end of your life—imagine for a moment that you are laying on your deathbed and you know that you are about to die. Reflecting on your past life:

What would be your greatest satisfactions? List at least three.

What would be your greatest regrets? List at least three.

What legacy do you want to leave when you die? How do you want people to think of your life when they remember you?

As you reflect on the above three categories, your potential calling and the goals needed to reach it should emerge.

Exercise 13-5: Based on the above four categories (Exercises 13-1 through 13-4), what types of potential ministry might you pursue for the remainder of your career in ministry? (Please list potential ministry areas without judging if they are possible, and without considering how to develop the skills needed. This is simply a brainstorming list.)

Victory enables a pathway toward happiness and joy

Seligman notes that victory provides a pathway toward joy. Winning matters to most of us. And the book of Revelations reveals who wins. Through the ages, millions of Christians find joy in the knowledge that they run with winners. We accept suffering knowing that in spite of it, we win. Ministers pursue victory, and the certainty of victory produces joy. When (not if) you struggle with happiness and joy, we recommend reading the book of Revelation.

C (the conditions of life) enables a pathway toward happiness and joy

C (the conditions that ministers need to flourish in their call results from 1) identifying the right goals, and 2) pursuing the right goals the right way. Hopefully, the above exercises helped you identify the right goals for your calling. However, ministers sometimes pursue goals in a manner that torpedoes their ability to succeed.

Positive attitudes build resilience

Emmons & Crumpler, 2000) and Emmons & McCullough (2003) found that gratefulness on a regular basis stimulates a positive attitude and results in contentment. Seligman, Steen, Park and Peterson (2005) developed their own version of a gratefulness exercise in which they ask individuals to daily enumerate three good things that have happened during the day, and reasons why each event was good. Peterson (2006, 38-39) reports the following instructions for the "**Three Good Things**" exercise:

- At the end of each day, after dinner and before going to sleep, write down three things that went well during the day. Do this every night for a week. The three things you list can be relatively small in importance ("My husband picked up my favorite ice cream for dessert on the way home from work today") or relatively large in importance ("My sister just gave birth to a healthy baby boy").

- After each positive event on your list, answer in your own words the question "Why did this good thing happen?" For example, you might speculate that your husband picked up ice cream "because he can be really thoughtful" or because I remembered to call him from work and remind him to stop by the grocery store." When asked why your sister gave birth to a healthy baby boy, you might explain, "God was looking out for her" or "she did everything right during her pregnancy."

Peterson et. al. found that their subjects reported increased levels of happiness and decreased symptoms for depression for up to six months following the exercise. Seligman reports a significant reduction in nightmares after doing the exercise for as little as one week.

Exercise 13-6: Try the Peterson **"Three Good Things"** exercise daily for one week. What are your insights after one week?

An alternative "gratitude visit" exercise reported by Peterson (ibid, 31) follows:

Exercise 13-7: Think of all the people—parents, friends, teachers, coaches, teammates, employers, and so on—who have been especially kind to you but have never heard your express your gratitude.

- Write a gratitude letter to one of these individuals, describing in concrete terms why you feel grateful.
- If possible, deliver it personally and have the person read the letter in your presence. If this is not possible, then mail or fax the letter and follow it up with a phone call.

Positive attitudes stimulate agreeableness

Peterson (ibid, 40) offers the following exercise to increase positive attitudes on your team:

- Choose one of the ongoing groups to which you belong but of which you are not a leader. Without fanfare, resolve to be the best group member (teammate) during the next month that you can be. The characteristics of the group will dictate the details of how you should act, but one would think that being a good teammate requires:
- Show up, literally and metaphorically
- Stop whining or being disruptive of feeling jealous
- Do more than your share
- Volunteer without being prompted
- Spread praise
- Help the leader—and of course—accomplish goals.
- Keep track of what you did and how it made you feel. Dissent is still possible, however, dissent can occur only with sensitivity to others as a good group member.

Using signature strengths in new ways increases resilience

Peterson (ibid, 99) reports that individuals who used their strengths in new and novel ways not only increased their level of happiness, but the effect lasted for over six months. To identify your personality strengths, please reference *Transforming Personality: Spiritual Formation and the Five-Factor Model* outlined on page ii at the front of this book. Using the spiritual disciplines and personality assessment tools, this book and related software provide you with the ability to interpret the Five-Factor Personality Model to assess your personality, fruit of the Spirit, motivational gifts of the Spirit, ministry aptitudes, vocational aptitudes, and preferred styles of behaviors. The strengths listed include:

Assertive	Warm and sympathetic
Talkative	Friendly
Socially Active	Considerate
Creative	Helpful
Artistically cultured	Hard working
Reflective	Dutiful
Scientific Interest	Organized
Philosophical	

Over the next week, use each of your strengths in a new way every day.

CHAPTER 14

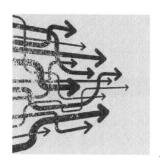

Emotional Resilience With The Right Goals

Transforming apathy into hope and resilience results from pursuing the right goals the right way. To pursue your goals the right way, we invite you to implement the following eight-step hope building process:

1. Reduce conflict between your goals.
2. Revise the goals that make you unhappy.
3. Refine your goals to promote emotional health.
4. Build two or more pathways toward each goal.
5. Build faith toward your goals.
6. Make goals and strivings realistic but just manageable.
7. Identify dual-purpose activities.
8. Look toward God to confirm your goals.

Reduce conflict between your goals

Pursuit of well-defined goals doesn't necessarily mean that you can accomplish them. Sometimes our goals conflict with each other.

Emmons (1999, 75) found that when our personal goals conflict with each other, the conflict frequently drives us toward burnout and depression. Emmons found that this aspect of goal development affects well-being more than any other characteristic about goals (Ibid., 60).

Goal conflict is defined as a situation in which the attainment of one goal interferes with the attainment of a second goal. Whenever our goals conflict with each other, we usually fail to accomplish either one. Snyder (2000, 113) states, "...the aim of psychotherapy is to remove these goal-blockages (and enhance hope) by increasing agency and providing effective pathways to desired goals."

Ministers often face at least three goal conflicts unique to their occupation:

A Sample of Daily Strivings

1. Spend quiet time with God.
2. Spend quality time with spouse.
3. Maintain a clean home.
4. Appear well-groomed.
5. Eat a healthy diet.
6. Exercise regularly.
7. Plan times of rest.
8. Plan for financial independence.
9. Care for my extended family.
10. Express appreciation to family and friends.
11. Find time to be alone.
12. Find time to study and learn.
13. Minister to others.

---

1. A minister may find a significant conflict between his or her ministry goals (such as sample strivings 1, 2, 6, 7, 11, 12, 13, below) and those that the extended family wishes him or her to adopt (such as striving number 9). More than other members of their immediate family, a minister is often viewed as the spiritual, emotional, and financial savior of their extended relatives. Since the minister preserves stable religious values, stable ethical values, and has learned interpersonal skills that enable him or her to deal with ambiguous situations such as cultural differences, the extended family may eventually recognize the value of the minister, and rely on him or her to resolve their problems. Almost every minister eventually experiences this particular goal conflict.

Thus, conflicting goals and strivings often arise when family members insist on elevating the minister into a role as a family leader. Although there is nothing inherently wrong with assuming the role as head of the extended family, the minister needs to make sure that he or she feels willing to pay the price financially, emotionally, and physically. Most ministers retain a very limited amount of energy and time available after pursuing their calling and other domains. The extended family may easily assume that the minister wants to meet all of their personal needs. After all, he or she possesses all the Fruit of the Spirit including kindness and compassion, right? So, they sometimes assume that the minister wants to meet the needs of the extended family even more than pursuit of ministry. Without strong personal boundaries, a minister may find that their personal and ministry goals conflict with goals to help the extended family. And when these goals conflict with each other and the conflict goes unresolved, the minister's goals rarely get accomplished.

In North America, almost everyone has access to Medicare and Social Security. I frequently hear a minister say, "If I don't care for my extended relatives, no one is there to do it." Usually, this represents a gross overstatement. Insurance, Medicare, Social Security, churches and community resources provide assistance to most of our relatives. Extended family members can sometimes offer care. Regardless, other sources almost always exist to provide care besides the minister. Nursing a chronic medical condition fatigues the best of care givers and can quickly undo your calling. Help your immediate family members find resources appropriate to their budget. However, guard yourself and your divine calling against those with goals which would conflict with your calling.

Conflicting goals may also arise when family members insist on becoming enmeshed in the minister's life. As parents and children become less able to care for themselves due to age, illness, disability, or personal crises, they may latch onto the minister, assuming that he or she feels duty-bound to care for them and meet their emotional and social needs. Indeed, most ministers really want to care for family members, especially for aging parents or struggling children. However, it is usually unwise to enmesh your life into someone else's life, much less the life of someone who needs chronic care. Many ministers deal with intense guilt over trying to retain personal space, time, and a debt-free lifestyle while caring for parents or children. Sometimes, the parents or children would like to ignore the minister's personal goals and boundaries, and sometimes the minister simply wants to offer care for them. Thus, an intense conflict develops between one's goal to care for relatives, and goals to maintain personal space, spiritual interests, and a calling into ministry.

2. Conflicting goals invariably arise when ministers remain at their assignment after sending their children away for an advanced education (such as college). Many children seem unprepared for independence. Regardless, minister parents still want to help their children. Thus, ministerial goals inevitably conflict with personal goals to nurture their children, especially as their children mature into college age adults. My (Nathan's) mother experienced her deepest depression after he returned to the States, alone, for college. She understood her 18 year old son's immaturity. Her goal conflict seemed almost too much to bear. For parents who want to give up during this time, I want to point out that their feelings are normal. Since 18 year old children possess legal freedom of choice, they invariably make good and bad choices regardless the proximity of their parents. Minister parents who blame themselves for their adult children's poor choices accept inappropriate blame. Minister parents share none of the blame when their adult children fail to seek their advice. With modern technology, wise parental advice remains only an e-mail or Skype call away. For myself, technology could not provide access to parental advice. However, I found surrogates who offered wise council. Hundreds of Christian parents will gladly offer wise council to any "preacher kid" (PK) or "missionary kid" (MK) who seeks it. The choice remains with each adult child, not the parent.

Differentiation from one's family of origin remains a hallmark of emotional maturity. If your goal to care for relatives and children conflicts with your personal or ministerial goals, carefully brainstorm and discuss the many options that preserve your personal space and goals even while helping your relatives and children. Enmeshment rarely offers a healthy option. Endeavor to maintain physical and emotional privacy even while caring for others. Without physical and emotional privacy, you risk depression. Once depressed, you will offer little care to others.

3. Conflicting goals invariably arise when PKs and MKs choose to reject God. Every minister wants their children to know God—a primary personal goal. When an adult PK rejects God and the minister couple subsequently keeps pursuing their ministry goals, an intense conflict arises between personal and ministry goals. Almost every minister couple faces this conflict, and it sometimes leads to ambivalent ministry and even attrition.

When a PK rejects God, most minister parents tend to blame themselves. However, the child retains a free will, and so parental self-blame represents inappropriate blame.

Most parents want to keep influencing their adult (eighteen year old) child. If their PK learned healthy differentiation, then their decision to accept or reject God results from a personal choice, independent from their parents. The parent can continue his or her calling knowing that the Holy Spirit will keep pursuing the PK in ways which the parent cannot understand.

I (Nathan) and my sister each rejected God by the time that we reached the age of eighteen. However, the Holy Spirit continued to pursue us. Today, we both feel proud that our parents remained in ministry.

Exercise 14-1: Please compare each of your goals to your other goals.

- What goal(s) might conflict with another?

- After identifying goal conflicts, brainstorm ways to reduce or eliminate conflicts. For instance, exercising regularly might conflict with maintaining a clean home since each activity requires time. One enterprising individual eliminated the conflict by cleaning the home while jazzercising to some lively music. Another individual found that spending time with her spouse conflicted with finding time to learn oil painting. However, she eliminated the conflict when she enlisted her husband in a class to learn their new hobby together.
- How can you reduce conflicts between your goals?

Emmons, Cheung, and Tehrani (1998) show that "spirituality fosters optimal health through a reduction of overall conflict [between goals]."

Revise the goals that make you unhappy

These are goals or strivings that, if you are successful, make you unhappy. For instance, you may want to pursue a goal to exercise one hour each day. However, if you hate to exercise, you may feel unhappy if you are successful at accomplishing that particular goal. Similarly, you may want to pursue a goal to eat a healthy diet. However, if you hate vegetables, you may feel unhappy at the prospect of eating a diet that includes vegetables.

Exercise 14-2: Honestly identify goals that will make you unhappy.

Brainstorm ways to make the goal, or activity, more enjoyable (e.g., if you hate to exercise, try doing it with a close friend; if you hate vegetables, get a new cookbook with interesting vegetable recipes). As a general rule, most individuals fail to retain goals very long if the goals create unhappiness. You will achieve your goals much more easily if you identify ways to make the activities enjoyable. How can you revise your goals to make them more enjoyable?

Refine your goals to enhance emotional health

Some types of goals remain emotionally unhealthy and simulate apathy, burnout, and even depression. Snyder (2000) offers the following research-proven guidelines to refine your goals.

State each of your goals in a *focused*, precise way. It is difficult to develop step-by-step plans toward vague goals. For instance:

Vague: "I want to serve as a missionary."

Focused: "I want to teach (a particular subject) in (a Bible School), in Kenya."

Similarly, many ministers aspire to the lofty goals of 1 Thessalonians 5, but never state them in a focused way. As we state the goals precisely, we can then develop step-by-step plans toward them.

Exercise 14-3: Looking at your goals, which goals can you now refine into a more focused and precise goal?

State your goals using positive terms instead of

negative terms. Negative goals seldom produce positive results. For instance:

Negative: "I want to argue less with other ministers and church members." You can achieve this by ceasing all communication with your peers. However, this approach fails to produce good communication and kills relationships.

Positive: "I want to develop better communication skills with my peers."

Exercise 14-4: How can you revise your goals in positive terms?

Develop approach goals instead of *avoidance* goals.

Avoidance goals seldom result in the intended benefit. For instance:

Avoidance: "I want to avoid unhealthy foods." Although one may avoid fatty bacon and candy bars, the resultant diet may also avoid fruits and vegetables. A diet based on avoidance may still remain quite unhealthy.

Approach: "I want a balanced and healthy diet for each meal."

Exercise 14-5: How can you revise your goals as approach goals?

Develop intrinsic goals instead of *extrinsic* goals. Intrinsic

goals are based on your internal values, shaped by God. Therefore, intrinsic goals usually energize you. Extrinsic goals seem more like obligations, and are based on someone else's values. For instance:

Extrinsic goal: "I will clean the office toilets because I am obligated to do whatever my supervisor tells me to do."

Intrinsic goal: "I want do this task because I am dedicated to becoming a servant like Christ. I am dedicated to tasks of service because I want to become more like Christ."

Exercise 14-6: Which goals can you refine as intrinsic goals rather than extrinsic?

Develop high value goals—ones that benefit the majority of

individuals over the few or yourself. High value goals benefit the majority of individuals, or, better yet, develop your skills so that you can benefit others. Most individuals feel energized when they perceive a broad benefit to their goals.

Exercise 14-7: How can you revise your goals to represent higher value goals?

Build two or more pathways toward each goal

Faith in a goal is defined as the belief that a goal remains attainable coupled with the energy to pursue one or more pathways toward that goal. James seems to agree, "You foolish person, do you want evidence that faith without deeds is useless? (James 2:20, NIV)

As expected, multiple pathways toward a goal usually generate more faith than a single pathway. That is, a higher likelihood exists that something might block a single pathway than two or more pathways. Thus, multiple pathways enhance faith by ensuring that the goal can be reached even though something or someone blocks a single pathway.

Frustration and apathy result when our goals seem firmly blocked (Snyder, 2000, 139). If someone feels apathetic, the person's apathy often results from blocked goals. Examine what blocks his or her goals. For instance, the apathetic "pew-sitter" usually retains one or more firmly blocked goals. With their goals blocked, they retain no reason to keep trying—apathy sets in. When apathy continues long enough, they give up all goals and not even recall his or her original goals, much less what blocked them. Sometimes this is called "learned helplessness."

Almost all pew sitters (and ministers) at some time in the past energetically pursued a ministry. As others differed with their service and blocked one or more of their goals, apathy set in. Thus, most individuals can benefit from building two or more pathways to each goal. If something or someone blocks one pathway, they can shift horizontally to implement an alternative pathway. And when we differ with a coworker, we can usually preserve their motivation more by helping them develop an alternative pathway instead of blocking their existing pathway.

Exercise 14-8: How have you noticed this principle working in your past, or in the past of another minister? Do you know ministers who have switched to a different ministry, changed ministry, or even quit ministry because their sole pathway to a goal was firmly blocked?

Many individuals report that they find it difficult to develop multiple pathways toward each goal. Some individuals report that this seems easier if they imagine watching themselves in a movie, performing the steps and sequence of events needed to accomplish each goal. To develop multiple pathways, imagine alternative ways to the same theme as if you were watching a movie. Consider making the pathways as concrete as possible—"the more specific the goals, the more likely they are to be attained", and "the clearer the steps are to a goal, the greater the likelihood of success (Snyder, 2000, 139)." Snyder suggests the following checklist (shown with permission) for developing your pathways (Ibid., 140):

√	Break each long-range goal into steps or sub-goals.
√	Begin your pursuit of a distant goal by concentrating on the first sub-goal.
√	Practice making different routes to your goals and select the best one.
√	In your mind, rehearse what you will need to do to attain your goal.
√	Mentally rehearse scripts for what you would do should you encounter a blockage.
√	Assume that you didn't use a workable strategy when you don't reach a goal, rather than harshly blaming yourself.
√	If you need a new skill to reach your goal, learn it.
√	Cultivate two-way friendships where you can give and get advice.
√	Be willing to ask for help when you don't know how to get to a desired goal.

Exercise 14-9: Consider how goal blockage affected your apathy in the past. Which of your current goals are most easily blocked? What is an alternative pathway toward each of your ministry goals?

Build faith toward your goals

Hope grows from three factors:
1. Multiple healthy goals (goals in each of the nine

domains).

2. Multiple pathways to accomplish each goal.
3. Faith—a belief that one can initiate and sustain the pathways, and energy to do so. For Christians, faith grows as we team with others, including God, and as we trust God to provide energy and resources.

Exercise 14-10: How will you develop a team of God and others to accomplish each of your God-given goals?

To whom will you be accountable to pursue the pathways?

For a Christian, faith building starts with dependence on God. Trust is most effectively built as we "look for hopeful stories" (Ibid., 140). Almost nothing increases faith more effectively than the testimonies of other Christians telling about God helping them through their time of difficulty. Snyder (Ibid., 141) also suggests the following checklist (shown with permission) for initiating and sustaining each pathway:

√	Tell yourself that you have chosen the goal, so it is your job to go after it. For a Christian, God probably chooses your goals, but you still retain the choice to accept it. Once you accept the goal that God lays on your heart, it is your job to pursue it.
√	Learn to talk to yourself in positive voices (e.g., I can do this! God will help me succeed).
√	Anticipate roadblocks that may happen.
√	Think of problems as challenges that arouse you. Go to God with your challenges—Don't let the challenges get the best of a goal that is God ordained.
√	Recall your previous *successful* goal pursuits, particularly when

	you were in a jam.
√	Laugh at yourself, especially if you encounter some impediment to your goal pursuits.
√	Find a substitute goal when the original goal is blocked solidly.
√	Enjoy the process of getting to your goals and do not focus only on the final attainment.
√	Focus on your physical health, including diet, sleep, physical exercise, and avoiding damaging substances (caffeine-laden products, alcohol).
√	Closely observe how God is working in your local world, including the little things happening all around you.

Make sure that your goals and strivings are realistic and just manageable

Due to crises or any number of physical or political problems, some previously held goals may no longer seem possible. If you can no longer accomplish your previous goals, substitute alternative goals. Continuing to pursue totally unreachable goals will merely cause a negative outlook on life. If you find that a goal is firmly blocked, adjust by finding an alternative goal. It is appropriate to grieve lost goals. It is also appropriate to move on to alternative ones.

If you are physically unable to accomplish a particular goal, is there someone else with whom you can team? Please discuss your goals with your leadership, with those whom you love, and with those who can function as mentors. Obtain ideas from as many sources as you can find.

Snyder (Ibid., 216) recommends setting goals that are just barely manageable. These goals tend to be the most rewarding because they "stretch" the individual to develop new skills and relationships. If you are unable to accomplish a particular goal, such as running a mile, substitute another goal that is just barely manageable, such as walking a mile.

Exercise 14-11: Consider the following to make your goals just manageable:

- If you develop a physical handicap, are you physically and emotionally unable to accomplish a goal, or can you team with someone else?
- If you are redefining your ministry role (such as transitioning to a new assignment), is each goal in line with your calling?
- Will you retain enough control to ensure that you can accomplish each new goal? What are some potential pathways to gain the needed control?
- How will you develop a team to help you reach each goal, or how can you join an existing team who shares the goal?

Identify dual-purpose activities

These are activities that enable one to pursue two or more goals through a single activity. For instance, if you engage in daily physical exercise with a friend or spouse, you might simultaneously reach your goals for health and fitness while also reaching your goals for a closer relationship. Alternatively, if you and a friend jointly pursue an academic goal together, you might simultaneously build a stronger relationship while achieving your academic goal. Can you identify some other ways that a single activity could serve your goals in two or more domains? Generally, it is very difficult to find enough time in a 24-hour day to accomplish one's goals across all nine domains unless you identify dual-purpose activities. Find and develop as many dual-purpose activities as possible. Otherwise, you probably will not have enough time to accomplish all your goals, and you may set yourself up for failure.

Exercise 14-12: What potential dual-purpose activities can you pursue that accomplish two or more goals at once?

Look toward God to confirm your goals

Exercise 14-13: How has God started confirming (through open doors, Scripture, answered prayer, other individuals, etc.) your goals?

Closing thoughts:

Emmons shows that we obtain more pleasure from making progress toward our goals than we do from achieving them. Pursuing the strivings related to our divine call provides more than happiness. It provides joy.

May God bless you as you intentionally refine your goals and pursue strivings related to your call.

PART IV:

How to Build

Spiritual Resilience

Spiritual Resilience—What is it?

The book of Psalms shows that the first step to rebound from depression, a downcast spirit, or a poor spirit starts with trusting in the Lord. Psalm 147:3 says, "He heals the brokenhearted, and binds up their wounds." Psalm 57:1 says; "For in you my soul takes refuge; in the shadow of your wings I will take refuge until the destroying storms pass by." Thus, King David shows that reliance on the Lord lets Him redefine a new normal for us. In the end, all resilience seems meaningless without spiritual resilience.

Relying on the Lord occurs numerous ways. It requires discarding dishonest and carnal ways in preference to thinking truthfully. It requires finding things for which we can feel thankful, daily, even in the midst of suffering. It requires reframing our suffering into hope just as Jesus reframed His suffering on the cross to look forward to resurrection. It requires pursuing a daily time of devotion and communion with God.

Spiritual Resilience Assessment

Score the below items as a 0, 1, 3, or 5, indicating the degree to which the statement characterizes you.

0 = this almost never characterizes me

1 = this characterizes me a little.

3 = this characterizes me somewhat.

5 = this characterizes me quite a bit.

Assessment A

	I have a lot of things for which to feel thankful.
	My ministry brings a feeling of meaningfulness into my life.
	I tend to stand in awe of what God is doing.
	When I see others around me, I tend to feel very fortunate.
	I feel fortunate for my friendships.

	I recognize times that God has allowed bad things to happen to me in order to help shape my life in a positive way.
	I cannot control some things that happen to me.
	I feel basically unsafe in this world even though my destiny remains safe in God.

_____ Total A Score

Assessment B

	I worry more than most individuals.
	I envy others, especially successful ministers.
	I tend to see things more skeptically than most people.
	I tend to be more disagreeable than most people.
	I am more impatient that most people.

_____ Total B Score

How to score your physical resilience self-assessment

Total the scores from your assessment A items to find your Total A Score. Total the scores from your assessment B items to find your Total B Score. Subtract your Total B Score from your Total A Score to obtain your Spiritual Resilience Score.

Total A Score - Total B Score = Spiritual Resilience Score

If your spiritual resilience score is:

0-19 = Your spiritual resilience is seriously degraded. You are highly susceptible to a spiritual crisis. You can benefit significantly from this section.

20-30 = Your spiritual resilience is marginal. Only one or two crises may stimulate a spiritual crisis. You can benefit from some chapters in this section.

31-40 = Your spiritual resilience is fairly good at this time. Please read the following chapters to better understand how to keep yourself spiritually resilient.

Part IV discusses the following factors that build hardiness against a spiritual crisis:

- Thinking truthfully
- Strengthening your call to ministry
- Practicing thankfulness and gratitude
- Turning suffering into hope
- Building a Godly personality

For additional information on these factors, please see:

Burns, David D. *The Feeling Good Handbook*. New York: Plume: 1999.

Emmons, R.A. *The psychology of ultimate concerns*. New York: Guilford Press, 1999.

Davis, N. W. and Davis, B. J. *Transforming Personality: Spiritual Formation and the Five-Factor Model*, projected publication in 2013.

CHAPTER 15

Using Truthful Thinking to Build Resilience

Thought distortions, perhaps more than overt lies, represent the most common pattern of (covert) lying that Christians use to deceive themselves and others. Some individuals lie by intentionally distorting the truth to more forcefully make a point. Other individuals fall into an unintentional habit that still distorts the truth. Thought distortions also undermine hopeful thinking. That is, research shows that thought distortions characterize depression. However, hope and distorted thoughts are mutually exclusive. That is, as we eliminate distorted thoughts we enable hopeful thinking and reduce depression.

The Apostle Paul challenges believers to recognize and work on their distorted thoughts. In 2 Corinthians 10:4-6, he encourages believers to "take captive every thought." His teaching in Ephesians 4:25-27 states: "Therefore each of you must put off falsehood and speak truthfully to his neighbor, for we are all members of one body. 'In your anger do not sin.' Do not let the sun go down while you are still angry, and do not give the devil a foothold." In secular society, lying is wrong; in the Christian community, followers want to avoid the smallest perception of untruth, even in their thought patterns.

In Matthew 15:17-20, Jesus highlighted the significance of the thought life:

> Don't you see that whatever enters the mouth goes into the stomach and then out of the body? But the things that come out of the mouth come from the heart, and these make a man "unclean." For out of the heart come evil thoughts, murder, adultery, sexual immorality, theft, false testimony, slander. These are what make a man "unclean;" but eating with unwashed hands does not make him "unclean.

Psychological research supports biblical teaching. Dozens of thought distortions exist. The most common thought distortions may be easily remembered by the statement, "Stop BOMBING your friends."

- Blaming
- Overstating
- Mind reading
- Branding
- Imperative statements
- Negative interpretation
- Guessing fortunes

Blaming

In many cases, blaming appears to be the easiest way to deal with tough and touchy issues. Rather than taking time to discover the cause of a communication breakdown, for instance, it may seem more expedient to blame one individual for a system-wide problem.

Focusing on blame is a bad idea because it inhibits our ability to learn what's really causing the problem and to do anything meaningful to correct it. The urge to blame is based, quite literally, on a misunderstanding of what has given rise to the issues between you and the other person, and on the fear of being blamed (Stone, Patton, and Heen, 59).

> It's the area director's fault that this project failed.

> I know. The rest of us certainly didn't do anything.

The recipient of blame will most likely feel judgment, which then can turn into defensiveness. Because defensiveness blocks meaningful dialog, it rarely has the desired effect. Without a meaningful dialog, the attacker simply ignores the excuse and attacks even more. The attacker will frequently take the moral ground once defensiveness happens.

Among the communication practices most detrimental to Christian maturity, Paul warned the Corinthian church about the danger of judging others: "Therefore judge nothing before the appointed time; wait till the Lord comes. He will bring to light what is hidden in darkness and will expose the motives of men's hearts. At that time each will receive his praise from God" (1 Cor. 4:5). In this Scripture, Paul referred to the Corinthians' pattern of comparing and contrasting God's people for their own judgmental purposes. "His command here should not be taken out of that context. Thus, 'before the appointed time' refers to the predilection of the Corinthians to judge from a human perspective, a mistaken tendency not to think eschatologically in terms of God's ultimate values (Soards, 89)." Humankind continues to struggle with the temptation to judge others. God views this practice as sin; He alone understands the human heart and its motives.

Most individuals struggle to understand their own motives, let alone the motives of others. God alone accurately judges both the conscious and unconscious dimensions of human activity.

The result of blame and the pain that it produces often causes individuals to withdraw or isolate themselves from others. The New Testament models community and teamwork. When team members engage in blaming, they lose the ability to see how they may have contributed to the problem. Blaming another person when something goes wrong prohibits the team from functioning at its best.

Blaming distorts the truth—it assumes that only one party is responsible for whatever is wrong. The fact is, each minister serves as a member of a team, and sometimes they are members of several teams. Even if they work alone, they still belong to a local team as well as an agency team. Team members are responsible for each other. For instance, when one spouse charges $10,000 on a credit card, both spouses remain responsible for the debt. Similarly, both spouses are responsible to discuss and set up boundaries on the use of their credit card. If either spouse spends too much money, the credit company will rarely place the blame on one spouse, but will require both to pay the bill. The same principle holds for interpersonal relationships. When a problem occurs, each member of a team shares the blame. Sometimes blame is simply the omission of setting up proper boundaries for the actions of each team member. Regardless, the blame is still shared. The sin of omission fails to exempt anyone from the consequences.

We recently spent many hours counseling couples in a country in which the missionaries regularly got together to blame their leader for their problems. Indeed, their leader had some personal problems, including clinical depression. By focusing on him, they omitted trying to find ways that they could help resolve their problems. After many years of blaming their leader, they finally started to see that they were part of a team. They took responsibility for the field problems, started seeking ways to resolve their problems, and even found help for their leader. Unfortunately, the early field relationships were built solely on finding fault with their leader. When he recovered, nothing positive remained to keep them together, and their friendships fell apart. The act of blaming distorted the truth, blocked their ability to solve problems, and prevented the growth of healthy relationships. This same story has been reenacted in a dozen different places. Some ministers are more adept at finding blame than in finding solutions.

Exercise 15-1: In what ways do you tend to engage in blaming? Who do you tend to blame the most often?

Overstating

Overstating (also called over-generalizing) uses one fact or event to generalize into a global rule. An overstatement assumes that things will always be a certain way. Sometimes, overstating classifies others as incompetent. This thought distortion appears in interpersonal communication with words such as always, never, and every. An example in the work place might be, "You never arrive on time," or "You are always late," or "Everyone does this." Global words such as always, never, and every, when used negatively in conversations, fail to give hope for change or growth. Overstating, in fact, does not represent truth. "Always" statements are almost always wrong, and "never" statements are almost never right. This deception creates a filter to authentic interpersonal communication (Schiraldi, 1999).

Overstating tends to attribute problems to other individual's character rather than their behavior. When you over-generalize to their character, you limit their control and limit solutions. Instead of overgeneralization, identify the behavior that bothers you.

I (Nathan) was recently confronted by a supervisor who used overstatements to justify his decisions. He said, "All of the [every one of the] other supervisors unanimously approved ...." His overstatement failed to acknowledge that some of them felt coerced to agree with him. His overstatement failed to acknowledge that regardless of what others approved, several valued a path of grace more than the approach that they felt coerced to accept. His overstatement failed to acknowledge that privately some of them worried about their decision. While polling the team members provides appropriate information, overstatements usually mask the truth.

When intentional, an overstatement is a lie. Some call it an "evangelistic lie." Some individuals use overstatements to more forcefully make their point. When unintentional, such as when used in error to generalize into a global rule, an overstatement still represents an untruth.

Exercise 15-2: Instead of accessing the playlist referenced previously in this book, for this chapter please access the video clips offered on a YouTube playlist at

http://youtube.com/playlist?list=PLB3CBEE0AFC273A99

Please view the video clip titled "Overstatement?" In what ways do you tend to engage in overstating?

Mind Reading

"Mind reading" represents another form of deception. Individuals engage in mind reading when they believe they know what another person is thinking. The distortion of mind reading inhibits clear interpersonal communication. Instead, mind readers assume that they understand the thoughts, beliefs, and motives of others. For the most part, these interpretations lean toward negativity. Thus, we tend to give ourselves the benefit of the doubt but assume the worst about someone else. For instance, it is common to think that a late individual doesn't care about the person he is meeting, while in fact, he may care greatly but has a legitimate reason for his delay.

Mind reading commonly appears in conversations that begin with "he thinks" or "she believes." Sadly, the individuals in question are not part of the conversation. No one can know another person's thoughts. Without taking time for questions and clarification, mind readers create barriers to clear communication (Stanley, McCain, and Trathen, 1996). The most dangerous mind reading occurs when individuals assume the following:

> bad behavior = bad intentions,
> bad intentions = bad character.

Once this thinking pattern is adopted, an easy leap is made from bad behavior to bad character. Fortunately, bad behavior is NOT always caused by bad intentions. The behavior may be a simple mistake, a result of something that is uncontrollable, or an oversight.

Mind reading continues when someone tries to mind read another individual's intentions. Without overtly asking about someone's intentions, they make assumptions that are often incorrect. Notably, the other individual usually values the behavior that others perceive as negative behavior. So, they evaluate that same behavior in a positive light. For instance, when a co-worker is late for a meeting, it is easy to employ mind reading and assume that the individual meant to miss the first portion of the meeting. Once you accept that someone has bad intentions, it is even easier to assume that the bad intentions result from a character flaw (he only cares about himself).

However, any number of justifiable reasons—cultural values, train crossings, meetings with supervisors—could account for a late arrival.

Usually, other's intentions are not negative. Most individuals simply jump to a negative judgment when they evaluate another individual's intentions. And, as they make that assumption, they have no way of knowing anything about the other individual's positive intentions unless they ask them, face-to-face. Thus, mind reading is inherently biased to the negative.

Since expectations are causative, mind reading is especially dangerous. When you mind read negatively, you risk causing others to react in a negative way due to your negative expectation. Due to the power of expectations, negative mind reading tends to become self-fulfilling. The key to ending mind reading is to stop focusing on what others think about you, and instead, focus on what you think about others. Ask and clarify their intentions.

Exercise 15-3: What behaviors characterize mind reading on the YouTube video clip "Mind Reading" on the playlist referenced on page 174? In what ways do you tend to engage in mind reading?

Branding

Is lunch ready?

You men are like placemats—you only show up when it's time to eat.

Branding, more often called labeling, is almost always a lie. Positive labeling, such as calling someone "perfect," creates unrealistic expectations. In truth, no one performs perfectly all the time. Negative labeling, on the other hand, is character assassination. Examples of negative labeling include terms such as jerk, idiot, and worthless. "When someone does something that rubs you the wrong way, you may tell yourself: 'He's a jerk.' You see them as totally bad. This prompts you to feel hostile and hopeless about improving things and leaves little room for constructive communication (Burn, 1999)."

Labeling or name-calling attacks another person's character. It ignores the fact that God created every individual in His own image. Jesus addressed this in Matthew 5:22 when He warned His followers regarding the detrimental effect of calling someone *raca*. The words "you fool" (Matt. 5:22) represented the highest of insults in Jewish culture because the term carried moral connotations. "The Greek word *moros* (the origin of the English word 'moron'), indicates a person who consistently acts like an idiot. To treat one's brother with such contempt was to strip way his personal identity and wrongly make the person into something he or she was not" (Wilkins, 242-243).

The meaning of *raca,* in colloquial language might be close to the label, "empty headed" (Stamps, 1992). It is slanderous, and could result in being taken to the Sanhedrin in the time of Jesus, or to a civil court in the present day. Although that label represents name-calling, it is not as damaging as calling someone a fool. In contemporary culture, the term "fool" carries a light and almost comical meaning. It fails to address the issues to which Jesus was speaking. Dallas Willard suggests that "you fool" no longer captures the sense of what Jesus taught. The words now carry a meaning closer to the colloquial term, "twerp." "To brand someone 'fool' in this biblical sense was a violation of the soul so devastating, of such great harm, that, as Jesus saw it, would justify consigning the offender to the smoldering garbage dump of human existence" (Willard, 154). Calling someone a "fool" represents clear-cut character assassination. Labeling someone represents character judgment, and only God perceives an individual's true character. Clear communication demands that believers honor God by showing respect for His children.

Jesus understood the normal feelings of anger and even contempt.

However, He also knew the importance of learning to forgive and to turn away from the temptation to attack the character of another individual. Identity theft strips individuals of their personhood while at the same time ending the possibility of a future relationship. "Jesus reveals that the intent of the law is to nurture relationships. Jesus' disciples must have a daily urgency about maintaining the healthy life of their relationships. ... Anything we do that strips away the personal distinctiveness of a brother or sister is sin (Ibid, 242-243)."

Common examples of character assassination include statement such as:

He's a little funny—an odd fellow

Who's the clown that did this?

He/she's really a nerd, an airhead, a blond

Exercise 15-4: What behaviors characterize labeling in the video clip titled "Branding" on the YouTube playlist referenced on page 174? In what ways do you tend to engage in branding? Who do you tend to label the most?

Imperative Statements

You shouldn't use "should" statements.

I must stop scolding.

For many parents, raising children includes daily doses of imperative statements. Imperatives such as "should," "ought," "why," "have to," and "must" continue to invade adult vocabulary. Often individuals use these imperative statements unnecessarily or even wrongly. The word "should," for instance, derived from the old English word, *scouelde*, continues to carry shades of its original intent, "to scold"

(Mish, 1985).

However, appropriate imperatives speak volumes. Imperatives appear appropriate in three instances:

- to describe if-then statements: If you should do X, then Y should result. For instance, if you study hard, you should get good grades.

- to describe the result of a natural law: For instance, if you light a match to dynamite, it should explode

- to describe legal requirements: For instance, the school rules are that you should …, or should not….

However, when used in everyday conversations, imperatives become thought distortions that create defensiveness and abuse in interpersonal communication. Alternatives to imperatives include stating your preferences instead of the imperative. For instance, instead of saying, "You should do …, We recommend that you state your preference, "I would like you to …, or I wish you would…."

Exercise 15-5:   List the common imperative statements that you tend to use with your:

Spouse

Children

Parents

Siblings

Friends

Peers

Students

List the common imperative statements that you tend to use with yourself:

Appearance

Dress

Prevention

Work ethic

Diet

Exercise

Education

What behaviors characterize imperative statements in the video clip titled "Imperative" on the YouTube playlist? The type of imperative statements (should, ought, must, have to, need to, why) that I use most often are:

Negative Interpretation

Grandpa, how much does it cost now days to get married?

I don't know son, I'm still paying.

Negative interpretation occurs when a statement is twisted to include a negative meaning that the originator never desired. One of the most obvious communication changes is an increase in negative valuation and a decrease in positive valuation. Where once we praised the other's behaviors or ideas, we now criticize them. Often the behaviors have not changed significantly; what has changed is our way of looking at them (Burns, 1999). Negative interpretation undermines even the strongest relationships.

Scott Stanley suggests that negative interpretation indicates a severe relationship danger sign. "In a way, this danger sign reflects the fact that we are simply not as nice, not as polite, not as respectful, and not as tactful to those closest to us. Many studies suggest that the negative patterns are far more potent than the positive" (Stanley, McCain, and Trathen, 34). Negative interpretation, in this context, refers to assigning a negative meaning to another individual's words or actions. Negative interpretation rates as one of the most common, yet most detrimental thought distortions to relationship health (Stanley, McCain, and Trathen, 26-27)."

Three signs of negative interpretation include:

- Bad memories. When individuals interpret events negatively, they tend to mentally re-write events with a negative bias. By doing this, they recall their bad memories with greater detail than their good memories. And their good memories are biased with negative connotations. For instance, a missionary friend chose to resign rather than face the consequences of a forced termination. Although we enjoyed many trips and conferences with our friend, he recently retold his missionary career story, which excluded all of his good memories. He left the organization with a bad memory of even the good times in his career.

- Failed attempts to restore the relationship. When relationships experience minor trouble, one of the members will sometimes try to repair the strain through comedy, a silly action, socialization, apology, taking a break (take-five), or inserting a nervous laugh. In other words, one individual usually attempts to smooth over the ruffled feelings and restore the relationship. Negative interpretation, however blocks this attempt. Individuals engaging in negative interpretation do not even notice the attempts to repair the relationship.

- Rumination. Individuals who engage in negative interpretation sometimes tend to ruminate about the negative events. That is, they tend to mull the negative events over and over again in their mind. They become "stuck" on the negative event. Rumination is a major precursor to clinical depression (Cosmides & Tooby, 1999; Noles-Hoelsema & Morrow, 1991). When you find yourself ruminating over negative events, break the pattern:

If necessary, break off toxic relationships that feed on negative rumination. When conversations primarily focus on negative events they generate unhealthy relationships. They rarely last any longer than the negative stressors on which they ruminate. When negative rumination occurs, it is important to either force the conversation toward positive topics, or break the relationship. Negative rumination frequently occurs in combination with the thought distortions listed in this section. However, the combination of negative rumination and "blaming" probably most characterizes these relationships.

Use a time-consuming and mind-engaging activity to break rumination. This will block your mind from continuing on this dangerous path.

Some cultures seem to specialize in negative interpretation. A student from the Philippines explained a cultural norm in his country which he called a "crabbing" mentality. This describes a passive-aggressive behavior in which subordinates try to pull down their superiors. Other cultures value a despondent and fatalistic outlook. In northern climates, where the lack of sunshine during the winter months plagues many people with seasonal affective disorder, negative interpretation is rampant.

Exercise 15-6: What behaviors characterize negative interpretation in the video clips titled "Negative Interpretation" and "Negative Interpretation-2" on the YouTube playlist?

Exercise 15-7: What are some ways that negative interpretation applies to your culture?

What are some ways that you commonly engage in negative interpretation?

Guessing Fortunes

Fortune tellers predict the outcome of future events, when in fact no one knows the future. The Bible includes only negative statements about fortune tellers. Fortune telling includes both positive and negative statements. Positive fortune telling might be, "If you make positive statements (positive confession) about yourself, God will make it come true." The statement may come true if you are lucky or if God chooses to intervene, but positive fortune telling probably angers God more than it controls Him. In spite of the fact that His Word has plenty of prohibitions against fortune telling, some ministers tend to treat it as a sacred act. While the Bible lists prophecy as a gift, it also includes four times as many warnings about abusing the gift than statements to encourage it.

> I feel tired today and I know I'll never get any better.

The Bible warns us to stone the false prophet. A positive outlook is emotionally healthy. Positive fortune telling goes beyond a positive outlook to a sacrilegious formula that purports to control God's intervention.

An example of a negative fortune telling would be, "Because he is not a good student, he'll never finish college." Positive and negative fortune telling fail to be truthful, and as individuals engage in this activity, their assumptions often prove to be inaccurate (Schiraldi, 38-45). At the same time, when you state a negative fortune to yourself, it tends to become self-fulfilling. If you state, "I feel tired today and I know that I'll never get any better," your negative self-image may help to fulfill your bad fortune. Whether positive or negative, clothed in "God-talk" or "self-talk," fortune telling is merely one more way that Christians sometimes lie to themselves and to others.

The human journey includes a struggle with thought distortions. Yet, with increasing awareness, believers may learn to pay attention to their thoughts and take steps to control them. Christians face the daily challenge to think, speak, and ultimately live in an ever-increasing awareness of truth.

What to Do about BOMBING

Most individuals struggle with one or more of the BOMBING thought distortions. Although it is easy enough to identify the thought distortions in others, it is much more difficult to detect them within yourself. However, with diligence, you can gradually eliminate these habits. It requires patience and five to ten years of consistent practice to overcome them. We recommend the following methods for eliminating thought distortions:

Since it is difficult to notice the thought distortions within oneself, give an accountability partner permission to help you identify them. Provide a small but meaningful reward to your partner whenever he or she identifies one of your thought distortions.

Notably, most individuals internalize what they teach. So, one of the best ways to eliminate the thought distortions is by teaching them to others.

Make a game out of it. Learn to recognize thought distortions with your peers or family members. Even if they are unaware of your game, reward yourself every time you discover someone using a thought distortion. By sensitizing yourself to others, you will more readily recognize them within yourself.

Daily ask God to help you eliminate thought distortions. Since He specializes in truth, He will help in ways that are beyond your own means.

Lastly, learn more about thought distortions and other relationship skills by practicing the skills outlined in *Transforming Conflict: Relationship Skills for Ministry*. This book represents volume 2 in the Living Well Series outlined on page ii at the front of this book.

Exercise 15-8: Please note that humor is often based on the thought distortions. Even though a distortion may be humorous, it has the potential to hurt others. The following list is indeed humorous, but it will give you practice at identifying everyday thought distortions. Please identify the distorted thought in each of the following statements (Steven Wright internet website quotes):

1. I'd kill for a Nobel Peace Prize.
2. Borrow money from pessimists—they don't expect it back.
3. Half the people you know are below average.

4. 99% of lawyers give the rest a bad name.

5. 42.7% of all statistics are made up on the spot.

6. A clear conscience is usually the sign of a bad memory.

7. If you want the rainbow, you have to put up with the rain.

8. I almost had a psychic girlfriend, but she left me before we met.

9. If everything seems to be going well, you have overlooked something.

10. Depression is merely anger without enthusiasm.

11. When everything is coming your way, you're in the wrong lane.

12. Ambition is a poor excuse for not having enough sense to be lazy.

13. Eagles may soar, but weasels don't get sucked into jet engines.

14. What happens if you get scared half to death twice?

15. Why do psychics have to ask you for your name?

Exercise 15-9:

- Describe the thought distortions shown in the video clip titled "Bombing" on the YouTube playlist.

- Describe the thought distortions your team members most often use.

- What are some ways to start eliminating your thought distortions?

- Without acting condescending, what are some ways to help your team members with their thought distortions?

Exercise 15-10: What are some ways that Christians commonly implement the BOMBING distortions in their relationship with God?

- Blaming—
- Overstating—
- Mind reading—

- Branding—
- Imperative statements—
- Negative interpretation—
- Guessing fortunes—

For more information on thought distortions and relationship skills, please see *Transforming Conflict: Relationship Skills for Ministers* referenced at the front of this book on page ii.

CHAPTER 16

Using Your "Ministry Call" to Build Resilience

In 1930, Watty Piper wrote a children's book (*The Little Engine That Could*) about a fictitious train engine that believed that she could climb a steep mountain to bring a load of toys and good food to good little boys and girls. The short children's story perhaps illustrates the concept of self-efficacy better than any highly funded research study:

> The very little engine looked up and saw the tears in the dolls' eyes. And she thought of the good little boys and girls on the other side of the mountain who would not have any toys or good food unless she helped. Then she said, "I think I can. I think I can. I think I can (Watty Piper, 1930)."

The "little engine that could" believed in her call so much that she persistently worked until she succeeded in climbing the mountain. In this children's book, Piper describes a belief so powerful that it often motivates children and adults alike into lifelong action. The concept of "the call" deals with a truth so simple that even a small child can understand it—when equipped with an unshakable faith in one's goals and ability, there are few limits to what one can accomplish. For ministers, the call encompasses this same belief. Just like the call felt by "the little engine that could," this call provides *the* most significant motivation for ministers.

Mary, the mother of Jesus, immediately understood the call when visited by an angel. Luke 1:38 records her simple, but direct, answer to God's call for her to bear the Son of the Most High. "I am the Lord's servant," she answered. "May it be to me as you have said" (NIV). Each Christmas, Mary's response continues to ring in the ears of ministers who study the power of the call.

The "call" builds identity

In *The Psychology of Ultimate Concerns* (1999, p. 5), Robert Emmons defines spirituality as a search for meaning, unity, connectedness, transcendence, and the highest of human potential. Since the call encompasses all these constructs and much more, it perhaps represents the bedrock of a minister's identity.

Emmons (Ibid., p. 3) asks, "What makes life meaningful, valuable, and purposeful? Goals provide a sense of meaning and purpose in life; without goals, it is difficult to imagine how one could lead a life that is meaningful and valuable." For ministers, goals result directly from a call. Thus, the concept of goals and a call become almost synonymous. Without a call, goals possess no meaning. Without goals, a call remains nothing more than an urge—meaningless by itself. For ministers, the call and goals operate hand-in-glove.

In a 1998 study, Emmons, Cheung, and Tehrani looked at the relationship between spiritual strivings (strivings that result directly from the call), emotional well-being, and overall life satisfaction. They addressed several questions about spirituality as related to "the call."

1. Can spirituality be reliably assessed through personal goals and strivings (that is, by following one's call)?
2. If so, do spiritual strivings (following one's call) increase a sense of well-being?
3. Are spiritual strivings (what results from a divine call) valued differently than non-spiritual strivings?

For question 1, the answer was yes. They found that personal spiritual goals result from one's spiritual calling. Individuals actively reorganized their daily strivings and long-range goals as a consequence of their spiritual calling and beliefs. To some degree, spirituality is measurable through spiritual goals and daily strivings.

For question 2, the answer was yes. Spiritual strivings were significantly related to higher levels of well-being, especially to greater purpose in life and to both marital and overall life satisfaction. The correlations between spiritual strivings and well-being were stronger than any other type of striving that had been studied. They found that "the call" brings contentment.

For question 3, the answer was yes. Spiritual strivings were rated as more important and requiring more effort. Individuals pursued spiritual strivings for more intrinsic reasons while they pursued non-spiritual strivings for extrinsic reasons. Spiritual strivings were associated with lower levels of goal conflict. Those with spiritual strivings set goals that were more difficult to achieve and showed higher levels of internal motivation and commitment.

Thus, when it comes to well-being, "all goals are not created equal" (Ryan et al., 1996, p. 7). Emmons concludes, "When people orient their lives around the attainment of spiritual ends, they tend to experience their lives as worthwhile, unified, and meaningful." In summary, Emmons et. al. show that responding to the call results in increased spirituality, higher levels of well-being, and greater life satisfaction.

Emmons concludes,

"… one needs to consider what is most essential to spiritual strivings. They may have an empowering function; individuals are more likely to persevere in these strivings, even under difficult circumstances. … Perhaps the most important function of spirituality [and the call] … is that it potentially can confer coherence upon the personality" (p. 108).

Davidson & Caddell (1994) further emphasize the importance of "the call:"

Personal strivings in life can become sanctified or imbued with a sense of the holy. As a consequence, they are likely to be appraised differently than are secularized strivings. When work is seen as a calling rather than a job, or as an opportunity to serve God, work-related strivings take on new significance.

The hallmark of psychological health is integration of the individual's personal and spiritual life. The call operates as the ultimate means to integrate the spiritual life with practical, concrete goals and daily strivings.

C. S. Lewis seems to agree (1960) stating that if God is at the hub of people's lives, the spokes of the wheel cannot other than be at perfect alignment with each other.

Mary, mother of Jesus, scarcely knew the joys or horrors that lay ahead. She simply answered, "I am the Lord's servant." However, the call integrated her life. In spite of the painful toil of fleeing to Egypt and watching her son experience rejection, hatred, and a wrongful death, she provides a picture of psychological health. The acceptance of God's call integrated Mary's life and produced psychological health even during the most stressful crises. Through seemingly impossible circumstances, Mary persisted. She possessed what modern research calls, self-efficacy.

What is God calling you to do?

Exercise 16-1: God is calling me to:

-
-
-

The call builds self-efficacy

Self-efficacy is not a skill that is developed or a genetically endowed trait that parents pass on to their children. Self-efficacy "is what I believe I can do with my skills under certain conditions" (Snyder and Lopez, 2002, p. 278). Thus, self-efficacy is a belief that you process the ability to succeed.

Exercise 16-2: On a scale of 1-10, with 1 representing almost no self-efficacy, 5 representing the self-efficacy of an average minister, and 10 representing the most self-efficacy possible, how much self-efficacy do you currently possess to accomplish your call? (That is, how much do you believe you can succeed?)

The call directly increases self-efficacy and results in persistence.

Self-efficacy motivates individuals to try harder and persist until they succeed. Thus, a minister who believes in his or her ability to accomplish the call has a great deal of self-efficacy, and the minister who doubts his or her ability has much less self-efficacy. Since *the little engine that could* said, "I think I can. I think I can. I think I can," she believed in her ability and therefore possessed a lot of self-efficacy. Due to her belief, she persisted until she succeeded. Just like the persistence of the "little engine that could," research supports that those with self-efficacy (a belief that they can succeed) persist and usually succeed.

Self-efficacy looks quite different for minsters than for secular individuals. For ministers, self-efficacy is: What I believe God will do through me under certain conditions and a belief that God will provide the ability to succeed in the tasks to which He calls me. Since the minister's definition avoids belief in oneself and substitutes a belief in God's ability, a minister's self-efficacy results in a confidence that he or she can accomplish otherwise impossible goals. For a minister, the call provides self-efficacy beyond anything remotely contemplated in secular society. The divine call provides God-based efficacy that transforms a secular individual into a minister who persists, knowing that God specializes in the impossible. In contrast to secular self-efficacy, Spirit-efficacy more appropriately describes the efficacy of a called minister.

A divine call confers the highest conceivable level of self-efficacy.

Much research supports the benefits of self-efficacy on emotional and physical health. As expected, self-efficacy (a belief in one's ability) greatly influences goal setting (Bandura, 1986). That is, humans tend to set higher goals when they believe that success is probable. When we possess self-efficacy, we persevere to attain difficult goals. Thus, the minister with a divine call knows beyond reason that he or she can attain even impossible goals, sets those goals, and therefore perseveres in spite of any hardships.

Mary, mother of Jesus, could not foresee the future. The birth of a child to a virgin didn't make sense. However, she possessed a divinely ordained certainty (Spirit-efficacy) that God who called her would accomplish the impossible. The Holy Spirit inspired a level of self-efficacy that seems totally absurd in secular society. A person without Spirit-efficacy would have said to the angel, "You're going to do *WHAT*? Yeah, sure!" Mary knew beyond reason that the impossible would soon happen. She possessed the highest conceivable level of self-efficacy.

Missouri is the "show me" state where residents proudly assert

> The little engine that could said, "I think I can. I think I can. I think I can." And, the little engine that could succeeded. The called minister says, "I know He will. I know He will. I know He will." And, God never fails.

that "seeing is believing." In contrast to needing to see what the future holds, Mary chose to persevere based on her call, not by sight. She felt compelled because she knew that God equips to accomplish His will. God provided Spirit-efficacy, a Spirit-led call that inspired and integrated Mary's entire life. Today, every Spirit-led minister follows in Mary's footsteps.

How can I strengthen my *respect* for the call?

A spiritual call originates only from God. However, God blesses all ministers with this gift.

Exercise 16-3: To strengthening your *respect* of the call:

- Intentionally plan goals and daily strivings to fulfill your call. As stated earlier, without goals a call remains nothing more than an urge—meaningless by itself. Enlist His insights to plan long-range goals and daily strivings that fulfill your call. What long-range goals and intermediate goals support your call?

- Ask for His plan to permeate your daily strivings. God provides us with a great gift—a new day every 24 hours to relate to others, work for Him, and worship Him. To strengthen your call, start each new day by asking Him, "What are your expectations today? What would you like us to do together today?" Once you align your expectations, your daily strivings quickly fall into place, supporting your call.

- Intentionally listen to God. God speaks to us in our quiet time with Him. We simply need to give Him that time and then listen. An infant approaches the father with constant babble and noise, which the father loves to hear. The mature adult listens to the Father, energized by His insights. To strengthen your call, schedule at least 20 minutes every morning and 20 minutes every evening to do nothing more than listen to Him. Maintain your devotional time but consecrate this listening time so devotional reading or study remains separate. As important as study is, time spent with God is perhaps more important than time spent reading about God.

- Seek input from spiritual mentors. James Maddux states, "Self and personality are socially embedded (in Snyder and Lopez, p. 279). The Bible states this more succinctly in Proverbs 15:22 (NIV), "Plans fail for lack of counsel, but with many advisers they succeed." Research and the Bible agree—others help us to better understand our calling as we gain input from them. List at least two individuals who can serve as mentors for your call.

- Design a monthly schedule to meet (or phone) each mentor to discuss your calling and plans for following your call.
    - Schedule for 1st mentor:

    - Schedule for 2nd mentor:

    - Schedule for other mentors:

How can I strengthen my *commitment* to the call?

Exercise 16-4: Please describe the following:
- What are the specific ways God has intervened to confirm

your previous callings? List at least three instances when you knew He called you to do something and then helped you to accomplish His will.

- If "seeing is believing," what can you see that God has already accomplished in relationship to your present calling? In what ways were His goals accomplished?

- List at least three opportunities God provided in the past to support your present calling.

- List at least two new opportunities that God is providing right now.

- List at least two relationships in which others help you directly to accomplish your call.

- Who helps you indirectly?

- How has God confirmed your call through loss and adversity?

- Can you control how to accomplish your call? How is God expanding your control over areas that enable you to accomplish your call?

- Imagine yourself accomplishing your call. What steps become evident? How is God enabling these steps?

- Who needs convincing about your call? After discussing this with God, what insights enable a persuasive argument to convince him or her?

- Describe how the call integrates all parts of your life (please use additional pages if necessary).

What is the power of the call in my life?

Exercise 16-5:   Reflect on the following statements thoughtfully and then write your answer.

- A minister who is called by God possesses enough power to … (insert an answer that God inspires in your heart).
- Due to the divine nature of my call, I personally have enough power to … (insert an answer that God inspires in your heart).

Exercise 16-6:   Rate the amount of self-efficacy you *now* possess as a result of completing the above exercises. On a scale of 1-10, with 1 representing almost no self-efficacy, 5 representing the self-efficacy of an average minister, and 10 representing the most self-efficacy possible, how much self-efficacy do you *now* possess to accomplish your call?

CHAPTER 17

Using Thankfulness
To Build Resilience

Someone recently asked me to define the opposite of thankfulness. Many individuals consider envy and covetousness as opposites to thankfulness. In some ways they are right. Psychologically, however, fear and thankfulness operate in a mutually exclusive manner. That is, recent research shows that the brain cannot physically process fear while simultaneously processing thankfulness. Thus, research and the Bible agree, "There is no fear in love. But perfect love drives out fear, because fear has to do with punishment. The one who fears is not made perfect in love" (1 John 4:18, NIV). Love produces thankfulness, which in turn excludes fear. So thankfulness operates as an antidote to fear. Ministers answer the call to service out of love. As their love for others builds, fear decreases. And as they develop thankfulness, they also feel less fearful.

Anxiety disorders routinely disable some ministers. Effective medications calm those with an anxiety disorder; however, thankfulness also calms anxiety. The spiritual exercise of counting one's blessings provides as much of an emotional lift as a spiritual lift.

Thankfulness: why is it important?

Emmons and McCullough (2003) looked at gratitude and thanksgiving in everyday life. For ten weeks, subjects were asked to complete a weekly log of their emotions, physical symptoms, and health behaviors. One-third of them were asked to simply record up to five major events or circumstances that most affected them during the week. One-third of the subjects were asked to write five hassles or minor stressors that occurred in their life in the past week. The final third were asked to write five things in their lives for which they were grateful. Additionally, they evaluated their life as a whole during the past week and their expectation for the upcoming week.

At the conclusion of ten weeks, the three groups showed significant differences. Relative to the hassles and events group, participants in the gratitude group felt better about their lives as a whole and were more optimistic about their expectations for the upcoming week. Over all, the thankful group reported fewer physical complaints than the hassles group and spent significantly more time exercising than the subjects in the other two groups. Please access the YouTube playlist referenced on page 31 and view the video titled "Robert Emmons: The Power of Gratitude."

Additionally, a daily gratitude intervention (self-guided exercise) resulted in higher reported levels of the positive states of alertness, enthusiasm, determination, attentiveness, and energy compared to a focus on hassles or a downward social comparison (ways in which participants thought they were better off than others). There was no difference in levels of unpleasant emotions reported in the three groups.

Participants in the daily gratitude condition were more likely to report having helped someone with a personal problem or having offered emotional support to another, relative to the hassles or social comparison condition.

The gratitude intervention seemed to cause an interesting side effect. At the beginning of the study, individuals were asked to write down six goals or projects they intended to pursue over the next two months. Two months later, they evaluated the degree of progress they had made on each of these six pursuits. Specifically, they were asked to rate how successful they had pursued their goals, noting how much progress they had made toward each goal and how satisfied they felt with their amount of progress. On average, participants who had been in the gratitude group reported making more progress toward their goals than participants in the other two groups. This fascinating finding suggests that the benefits of an attitude of gratitude extend beyond the domain of mood and well-being to encompass more specific indicators of successful living—the attainment of concrete goals in life. The study provides empirical confirmation of the saying that "thanksgiving leads to having more to give thanks for," and that there are benefits to "counting one's blessings, one by one" (Templeton, 1997).

In a follow-on study of adults with neuromuscular disease, a 21-day gratitude intervention resulted in greater amounts of high energy, positive moods, a greater sense of feeling connected to others, more optimistic ratings of one's life, and better sleep duration and sleep quality—relative to a control group.

Other important benefits of gratefulness include:

Well-Being: Grateful people report higher levels of positive emotions, life satisfaction, vitality, optimism, and lower levels of depression and stress. The disposition toward gratitude appears to enhance pleasant feeling states more than it diminishes unpleasant emotions. Grateful people do not deny or ignore the negative aspects of life.

Pro-sociality: People with a strong disposition toward gratitude have the capacity to be empathic and to take the perspective of others. They are rated as more generous and more helpful by people in their social networks (McCullough, Emmons, & Tsang, 2002).

Spirituality: Those who regularly attend religious services and engage in religious activities such as prayer (and reading religious material) are more likely to feel grateful. Grateful people are more likely to acknowledge a belief in the interconnectedness of all life and a commitment and responsibility to others (McCullough et. al., 2002).

Materialism: Grateful individuals place less importance on material goods. They are less likely to judge their own and others' success in terms of possessions accumulated, less envious of wealthy persons, and more likely to share their possessions, compared to less grateful persons.

Gratefulness: not the same as indebtedness

Ministers and especially missionaries sometimes report feelings of indebtedness to churches that support them, and even to God. In studying the difference between gratefulness and indebtedness, Gray & Emmons (2000) found that people who write about being indebted to others report higher levels of anger and lower levels of appreciation, happiness, and love—relative to people who write about being grateful. Additionally, the experience of indebtedness is less likely to lead to a desire to approach or make contact with others—relative to an experience of gratefulness. Thus, indebtedness tends to be an aversive psychological state that is quite different from gratitude. What are some ways that your feelings of indebtedness possibly stimulate a lower level of appreciation rather than feelings of gratitude?

Thankfulness: how to develop it

Mitchel Adler (2001) defines eight aspects of appreciation. To develop thankfulness, try the following eight-week program. By the end, you will discover deep feelings of thankfulness, be more appreciative of others, and sing praises to God.

Exercise 17-1: A positive statement, or thought, followed by a task is given for each day. Think about each statement and repeat it to yourself many times throughout the day. In some cases the thought may not seem to apply to your situation, especially if your thankfulness has degraded to feelings of indebtedness. Keep in mind that the statement does not have to describe you at the present time. If you can think of a single instance or episode where the statement applies, focus on that memory. Also try to complete the simple task that follows each positive statement. Make sure to complete the task for each day, no matter how you happen to feel that day. Do not stop even if horrible things have occurred.

Although this exercise might sound silly, it comes from a wide body of research. This approach is one of the tenets of cognitive therapy, which has proven highly successful. If, over time, you deliberately accustom your mind to thinking on the good things in life, your outlook will change. What Scriptures support this principle?

Week 1: Have focus—What do you *have* for which you feel appreciative? (Note that what you have is not only confined to material possessions but also includes possessions that are not tangible.)
Monday:

Thought: I am genuinely blessed by tangible things that God and others have provided.

Task: List your physical blessings in this world.
Tuesday:

Thought: I am blessed with opportunities.

Task: List the opportunities God has provided and write a paragraph about them.

Wednesday:

Thought: I am fortunate.

Task: Pick two things for which you are particularly fortunate and write a few sentences about them.

Thursday:

Thought: I am blessed with good things in life.

Task: List some good things that God provides that you particularly like.

Friday:

Thought: My coworkers have specific qualities that make me proud.

Task: Write down one characteristic of each coworker that makes you proud.

Describe your insights after **Week 1** of this exercise.

Week 2: *Awe*—What makes you sometimes stand in *awe*?

Monday:

Thought: I feel a genuine sense of awe at how God has guided my life and ministry.

Task: List the ways that God has guided your life and ministry.

Tuesday:

Thought: I am fortunate to be alive.

Task: List specific past events where God intervened to protect you and your family.

Wednesday:

Thought: I am in awe of how God has designed nature.

Task: List at least two things in nature that provide you with an emotional connection to God.

Thursday:

> Thought: I am blessed with miracles that God still is performing in my life and in the lives of those I love.
>
> Task: List some ways that God is still in the process of performing a miracle in your life and in the lives of your loved ones.

Friday:

> Thought: I am in awe of my coworkers.
>
> Task: How is the hand of God evident in His selection of the role of your coworkers in your life?

Describe your insights after **Week 2** of this exercise.

Week 3: Rituals—What specific acts or *rituals* do you use to give thanks to the Lord and to others?

Monday:

> Thought: God guides my life and ministry through the rituals that He has put in my live.
>
> Task: List the specific rituals or events that remind you to give thanks on a regular basis.

Tuesday:

> Thought: I want to purposefully give thanks to God.
>
> Task: List some ways that you can remind yourself purposefully to give thanks to God.

Wednesday:

> Thought: I want to purposefully give thanks to those I love.
>
> Task: List some ways that you can remind yourself purposefully to give thanks to your loved ones.

Thursday:

> Thought: I want to purposefully give thanks to those with whom I work.

Task: List some ways that you can remind yourself purposefully to give thanks to those with whom you work.

Friday:

Thought: I want to purposefully give thanks to those who dislike me or who hurt me.

Task: List some ways that you can remind yourself purposefully to give thanks to those who dislike you or hurt you.

Describe your insights after **Week 3** of this exercise.

Week 4: Present moment—In what ways do you stop to appreciate the *present moment* even while you are experiencing it?

Monday:

Thought: God gives me nature to enjoy every day.

Task: List at least two aspects of nature that I see every day but sometimes fail to stop and appreciate.

Tuesday:

Thought: God gives me wonderful work and ministry to enjoy every day.

Task: List at least two positive things about your work and ministry that you sometimes fail to stop and appreciate.

Wednesday

Thought: God gives me relationships to enjoy every day.

Task: List at least two things about the people in your everyday life that you sometimes fail to stop and appreciate.

Thursday:

Thought: God orchestrates wonderful events in my everyday life.

Task: List at least two events in your everyday life that you sometimes fail to stop and appreciate.

Friday:

Thought: God gives me wonderful leaders in my everyday life.

Task: List at least two ways that you sometimes fail to stop and appreciate your leaders.

Describe your insights after **Week 4** of this exercise.

Week 5: *Social comparison*s—By remembering some individuals who are less fortunate than yourself, are you periodically reminded to take note of your blessings?

Monday:

> Thought: God blesses me in comparison to the others around me.
>
> Task: List some ways that God blesses you in comparison to those in your adopted country.

Tuesday:

> Thought: God blesses me in comparison to my coworkers.
>
> Task: List some ways that God blesses you in comparison to those with whom you work.

Wednesday:

> Thought: God blesses me in comparison to my leaders.
>
> Task: List some ways that God blesses you in comparison to your leaders.

Thursday:

> Thought: God blesses me in comparison to my relatives.
>
> Task: List some ways that God blesses you in comparison to your relatives.

Friday:

> Thought: God blesses me in comparison to other ministers.
>
> Task: List some ways that God blesses you in comparison to other ministers.

Describe your insights after **Week 5** of this exercise.

Week 6: Gratitude—For what do you feel gratitude?

Monday:

       Thought: God blesses me with the sacrifices of others.

       Task: List the sacrifices that others have made on your behalf for which you are presently grateful.

Tuesday:

       Thought: Others bless me in ways that I can never repay.

       Task: List the emotional or monetary debts to others that you can never repay.

Wednesday:

       Thought: God blesses me with opportunities.

       Task: What are some of the opportunities you have experienced for which you feel grateful?

Thursday:

       Thought: God blesses me uniquely.

       Task: For what are you especially thankful to God (what has He done uniquely for you)?

Friday:

       Thought: God blesses me with love that I never earned.

       Task: List some ways that you receive love that you never earned.

Describe your insights after **Week 6** of this exercise.

Week 7: *Loss and adversity*—What personal *losses and adversities* have reminded you of how fortunate you really are?

Monday:

       Thought: God blesses me with personal problems.

       Task: What personal problems remind you to value the positive aspects of life?

Tuesday:

       Thought: God blesses me with challenges.

       Task: What personal challenges remind you to value the positive aspects of life?

Wednesday:

Thought: God blesses me with losses.

Task: What losses remind you to value life?

Thursday:

Thought: God blesses me with relationship conflict.

Task: What relationship struggles remind you to value others?

Friday:

Thought: God blesses me with adversity.

Task: What, in particular, reminds you to live every day to the fullest?

Describe your insights after **Week 7** of this exercise.

Week 8: *Interpersonal relationships*—For what interpersonal relationships are you appreciative?

Monday:

Thought: God blesses me with people who care and show commitment to my well-being.

Task: List the people who care about you.

Tuesday:

Thought: God blesses me with people who understand me.

Task: List the people who understand you.

Wednesday:

Thought: God blesses me with people who I like to be around.

Task: List the people who you like to be around.

Thursday:

Thought: God blesses me with people who mentor me.

Task: List the people who mentor you, sometimes even unknowingly.

Friday:

Thought: God blesses me with people who help me.

Task: List the people who serve interdependently with you.

Describe your insights after **Week 8** of this exercise.

CHAPTER 18

Using Hope And Suffering To Build Resilience

In 1943, fourteen year old Jim Davis caught tuberculosis, an almost certain death sentence at that time. No antibiotics yet existed for the terrible disease. He remembers hearing the local doctor tell his mother, Edith, that her son would almost certainly die. In a tuberculosis hospital, however, a visiting minister introduced him to the Bible. Following his conversion, Jim experienced instantaneous spiritual and physical healing. Sixty-one years later, he retired after serving 48 years as a foreign missionary. Today, Dr. Davis notes that, other than the decision to become a Christian, the suffering of tuberculosis brought the most positive results to his life. God helped him turn suffering into hope. And hope produced resilience over a lifetime of missionary service.

What's so sacred about hope?

Few individuals talk about hope except to note that the triad of faith, hope, and love includes hope as a lesser virtue. What's so sacred about hope? What makes hope so crucial for ministers?

The Apostle Paul lists hope as one of the big three virtues—"And now these three remain: faith, hope and love. But the greatest of these is love (1 Corinthians 13:13, NIV)." Since Paul lists love as the greatest virtue, ministers often teach about it instead of hope.

Due to their drive toward self-reliance, many modern Christians possibly value hope less than previous cultures. A 2005 Harris poll found that 47% of North Americans place their confidence in small business, 47% rely on the military, 38% rely on education, and 24% place confidence in organized religion.

In industrialized countries, crises happen but generally occur less frequently than elsewhere, and with some degree of financial and family support. For instance, North Americans and individuals in many industrialized countries enjoy the benefits of life, car, home, health, and bank insurance. The U.S. government provides Medicaid and Social Security for the elderly and disabled. When a national disaster strikes, the government helps. The government provides police and FBI for security. A large percentage of Christians flourish in a church community that also helps during a crisis. Thus, many Christians from industrialized countries simply don't need to look toward God as a source of hope. North American currency may say "In God we trust," but for some, their hope remains in small business, the military, education, a set of insurance plans, or a well-funded government bail-out package.

In contrast to those described above, many third world Christians persist only because of hope. We recently relearned this truth where we ministered in the Philippines after a series of typhoons. By the night of October 10, 2010, the typhoons had dumped 39 inches of rain on Baguio City. A young Christian, Antoinette Anablon Kindipan, feared for her life. She wrote on her Facebook blog, "Tonight, even as I write this, the rain continues to pour on. But what's good about it is that it makes me value more the thought that life is brief, that there are so many things to be thankful for, that I can always trust the One who gives life to spare my life and the ones I love from this storm."

Antoinette expressed hope (and trust) in God. As the rains continued the following night, the mountainside suddenly turned to liquid mud, killing her and her entire family in a massive mudslide.

A non-Christian would probably focus on the fact that hope failed to spare Antoinette from death. Christians, however, focus on Antoinette's choice to persist in hope, regardless the outcome. Like the hope that Jesus experienced on the cross, when faced with death, hope kept Antoinette going. For Antoinette and most third world Christians, hope sustains them during crises and suffering, regardless the outcome. They persist because of hope.

Jeren Rowell (2010) reports that nearly 40 percent of pastors that he surveyed have considered leaving vocational ministry during the past three years. When they reach the point that everything seems entirely hopeless, most ministers quit. That is, no one keeps working when everything seems absolutely hopeless. For instance, a missionary reflected that in 20 years of ministry, he never witnessed a single conversion to Christianity. Without hope of bringing others to Christ, he quit within the year.

While the "call" motivates a minister to go and serve, hope motivates a minister to stay.

As long as a minister can retain hope, he or she can persevere in spite of the worst dangers and crises. Love may represent the greatest virtue for a Christian (and most ministers act out of love), but that same minister cannot survive without hope. Just as hope serves as an antidote to the hardships of life, it also provides perseverance—a fundamental component of minister longevity.

Making sense of suffering builds hope

Martin Seligman states (2002, xi), "The positive emotions of confidence, hope, and trust, for example, serve us best not when life is easy, but when life is difficult." A resilient minister reframes suffering and uses it to build more resilience. Thus, hope helps each minister persevere through the worst of crises. The Apostle Paul states the principle of hope a little more clearly, "And we rejoice in the hope of the glory of God. Not only so, but we also rejoice in our sufferings, because we know that suffering produces perseverance; perseverance, character; and character, hope. And hope does not disappoint us, because God has poured out his love into our hearts by the Holy Spirit, whom he has given us" (Romans 5: 2-5, NIV). Seligman accurately notes that suffering produces perseverance. The Apostle Paul goes several steps further, observing that suffering produces perseverance, perseverance produces character, and character produces more hope.

Jonathan Haidt notes a primary function of suffering—humans *need* suffering to produce character. Although Romans 5:2-5 states that suffering produces character and hope, most Christians try their best to avoid it. For example, believers highly value passing their values onto their children. But which parent prays for their children to experience suffering to develop character and hope? Romans states that suffering produces perseverance; perseverance, character; and character, hope. But we don't know a single minister who asks God to send more suffering to stimulate his or his child's character development. If we really believe this Scripture, "We should take more chances and suffer more defeats. It means that we might be dangerously overprotecting our children, offering them lives of bland safety and too much counseling while depriving them of the 'critical incidents' that would help them to grow strong (Haidt, 141)."

And just as we prefer to offer our children lives of "bland safety," most of us also prefer that lifestyle for ourselves, rather than the stark reality of what we face in many ministries. Thus the safely contented and isolated minister possibly fails to grow.

It is through engagement with the normal critical incidents of life that each minister inevitably experiences suffering and pain. So suffering seems to operate as a fundamental component to produce character. Many avenues stimulate growth, but Christians *must* make sense of their suffering in order to grow from it. As we reflect and make sense of our suffering, we use the worst of life's stressors to build additional hope and resilience.

Exercise 18-1: To understand how suffering builds hope, explain how your theology of suffering has affected your beliefs in the five areas below:

- Some Christians believe that bad things can't happen to good people. How has your belief on this subject matured after experiencing the crises in your life? How has your experience corresponded to Job's? For instance, in my airplane incident related in Chapter 4, I found that bad things often happen to good people, including myself. God never spared me from a life-threatening plane crash. After a harrowing miss with death, we set down in an open field. Recognizing the high rate of death from similar incidents, I now believe that God spared me for a purpose. A belief in that purpose reframes an extremely negative incident into a positive experience. Thus, God may allow or even cause a bad experience in my life to shape me and influence my future pathways.

- Some Christians believe they always have the ability to control their environment and the conditions to which they are exposed. How has your belief on this subject matured after experiencing the crises in your life? How has your experience corresponded to the Apostle Stephen? For instance, in my (Nathan's) airplane incident related in

Chapter 4, I found that I cannot control many events that happen to me. God remains in control, but Christians merely trust that they will "be home" with Him some day. We never control Him, and often cannot control what happens to us. However, we can trust God to walk with us in our crises.

- Some Christians believe their destiny in this world remains almost totally up to their own actions. How has your belief on this subject matured after experiencing the crises in your life? How has your experience corresponded to the Apostle Stephen, King David, or the Apostle John?

- Some Christians believe that the world is a safe place and people are basically good. How has your belief on this subject matured after the crises in your life? How has your experience resembled Jonathan's, Kind David's closest friend?

- Some Christians believe that nothing good can result from their crisis. Many individuals especially cannot envision any good coming from a very recent crisis. Instead of arguing or trying to identify a good result for them, let them know that God will reveal it at a later date. Let them know that good can result from any crisis, but they may not recognize it for a while. For instance, Jim Davis contracted Parkinson's disease after serving 48 years as a missionary. Initially, he felt devastated at the thought of gradually losing his ability to minister. Six years later, however, he now reports that the disease acts as one of the more positive influences on his life. Although he spent his previous life "doing" ministry, he now spends most of his day with the Lord. He has developed a deeper relationship never possible in his previous lifestyle of "doing" ministry. He reports that he would never want to go back to his pre-Parkinson days.

CHAPTER 19

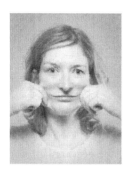

Building Resilient Character Traits

In 1996, we chose to initiate a very different lifestyle behavior than we had ever considered. We chose to spend twenty minutes alone with God every morning, immediately after breakfast, and another twenty minutes alone with God every evening, immediately after arriving home from work. One of our friends called it, "Listening Prayer." We selected separate places in our home, and initiated the twice-daily *connections*.

We considered this lifestyle as a trial. In this manner, we continued month after month until, to our surprise, an entire year lapsed. I (Nathan) never noticed any difference in our personal lives.

However, a little over twelve months after we started daily Listening Prayer, I noticed that my work environment drastically changed. For the first time in 28 years as a psychologist, my colleagues seemed to genuinely enjoy my company. For the first time in all those years, I arrived each morning to find my office already full of colleagues, waiting to discuss, of all things, biblical issues. I never tried to evangelize or steer the discussion in any way.

For a split second, I wondered about this change. Then, I wondered about the only lifestyle change that we had practiced during that same time period. After my colleagues departed for their own office that morning, I accessed a computer file with the five-factor personality assessment for the first time in over twelve months. I carefully and painstakingly answered each personality question as accurately and carefully as possible. Then, I took the assessment home and asked my wife to take the assessment, once again. The figure below shows our combined results, in comparison to our original scores.

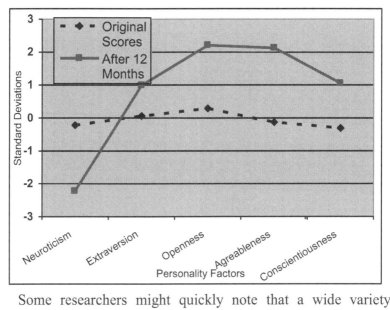

Some researchers might quickly note that a wide variety of environmental factors, other than Listening Prayer, could easily account for the observed personality changes. I agree. However, only two issues seem relevant to most Christians:

1. Did our relationship with God deepen during those twelve months?

2. Did the practice of spending time consistently in the presence of someone who is very different (God) make it difficult to maintain constancy in our personalities? That is, did God stimulate a change in our personalities?

We learned five fundamental truths from our personal journey:

1. Individuals who consistently spend time in the presence of God get to know Him. Previously, we read a lot about God, sometimes reading the Bible for hours at a time; but, we since we failed to spend much time with Him, we never knew Him intimately.

2. Individuals consistently in the presence of God develop a keen sense of His presence throughout the day. Although we initially spent only twenty minutes with Him, twice each day, after twelve months of this behavior, we sensed His presence constantly and noticed ourselves talking to Him throughout the day. For the first time in my life, God did not live somewhere in heaven. I felt His presence within me.

3. Individuals consistently in the presence of God are driven to become more like Him. As a result of therapy, personality can generally change at a rate of one-half of standard deviation per year, with a maximum change of about one standard deviation over an entire lifetime. Moreover, that rate and magnitude of change applies to only one personality factor. In contrast, we changed approximately two standard deviations on four out of five personality factors over a single twelve-month period. Such is the power of the Holy Spirit. We never pursued change as an objective. It resulted as a natural outcome of spending consistent time in the presence of someone (God) with a radically different personality.

4. Individuals consistently in the presence of God rarely notice any personal change, but others do. Ironically, neither of us

ever noticed any change in ourselves. However, our colleagues started to respond differently to each of us. They noticed the difference, first.

5. The fifth fundamental truth centered around a key question, "What happens if I stop spending time with God on a daily basis? Is spiritual growth and the resultant personality change temporary or permanent?"

We had listened to sermons in which the minister compared a new Christian to a young sapling, and compared the older Christian to a giant redwood. However, we have never encountered a redwood that shrank from its mature size to that of a sapling, so we assumed that spiritual growth probably remains permanent. Within a year after discovering the above truths, we moved to another state to raise financial support to become foreign missionaries. We filled our days with phoning pastors and driving hundreds of miles to preach at their churches.

One particular pastor showed keen interest in Listening Prayer and asked us to hold a seminar in his church. He wanted each individual to take the personality assessment. In preparation, I accessed the computer file with the five-factor assessment, and re-tested myself to make sure that the software functioned properly. Nothing seemed to work right. I slowly started stepping through each line of computer code, trying to find the problem. After about an hour, I found the problem—the software still worked perfectly, but the personality of the tester had changed so drastically that I no longer recognized my own personality profile.

As I reflected on the past four months of extremely productive ministry, I realized that in the midst of developing a new ministry, I had stopped spending time with God on a daily basis. In as little as four months, my personality had regressed to the point that it now looked exactly like it looked two years previously. All the personality change vanished. I looked like my old self. That day I learned a fifth fundamental truth of spiritual change: Change lasts only as long as we *persistently* spend time daily in the presence of God.

Although we had each noticed a few personal changes during our lives, as we started this journey our personalities looked amazingly like the average secular individual in North America. Although we knew that the Bible said that we could develop a new nature, our personality never reflected any change. We desperately wanted to exhibit the fruit of the Spirit, but the personality assessment showed that our Agreeableness Factor looked just like any other average individual. Additionally, a substantial body of research showed that we probably would not change.

Thus, the Holy Spirit seemed to cause us to change as we engaged in Listening Prayer—something we could not accomplish on our own. He instigated change, causing us to become more like Christ. We searched to see if this role seemed consistent in Scripture: ". . . from whom the whole body, supported and held together by its ligaments and sinews, grows as God causes it to grow" (Colossians 2:19). "But when he, the Spirit of truth, comes, he will guide you into all truth" (John 16:13). "His divine power has given us everything we need for life and godliness through our knowledge of him who called us by his own glory and goodness" (2 Peter 1:3).

Thus, the Holy Spirit causes change when we connect with God. That change builds the Kingdom of God, within each believer, one believer at a time. The Kingdom acts as something more than a heavenly kingdom; it is initiated on earth through the development and change within individual believers.

Also, please reflect on the role of the individual believer. That is, what was our role in the process of change? The Bible invites us to become holy. "Be holy even as I am holy" (Leviticus 19:2). To grow truly holy, as God is holy, we need to experience change. This kind of change involves more than a salvation experience. It is not a superficial change in which we continue to display unholy attitudes and behaviors that seem typical of the average person.

This kind of change involves not only outward behaviors, but it also includes feelings, attitudes, and every internal motive that separate us from Christ. However, we cannot change ourselves. Even secular research confirms that personality change remains difficult. However, we can choose to put ourselves in a place where the Holy Spirit can change us. That place is "in the presence of God." It is a spiritual walk in a new kind of Garden of Eden. It is a path where God invites us to walk, continually, with the Holy Spirit. "Be joyful always; pray continually" (1 Thessalonians 5:16-18). "Devote yourselves to prayer" (Colossians 4:2). This daily walk remains no less real than the evening strolls that Adam and Eve enjoyed with God. He invites us to walk alongside Him, getting to know Him. It is what God has desired ever since He created Adam and Eve.

Unless believers pray daily, they never "have a prayer" to grow. We never grow holiness through self-effort. It results from spending time with the One who is holy, letting Him convict and uniquely change us, as He desires. It is more than telling God what we want Him to do. And it is more than outward activity, including ministry. It is a result of choosing to walk daily in His presence.

Do not use lifestyle behaviors as a formula for freedom or as a means to cleanse from dysfunctions. These lifestyle behaviors are not meant to manipulate God. They are a way to KNOW God—the primary benefit. The secondary benefit is that if I spend time with God, one of us will change—guess who?

If I spend time with God, one of us will change— guess who?

Has God told us what to do? Yes, He tells us to meditate and pray continually. He tells us to put on a "new self" created to be like God.

Why meditate? The German theologian Dietrich Bonhoeffer

answered this simply, "Because I am a Christian." Walking in the presence of God remains central to development of the new self. To be a "Christian" means we are like Christ. It is inconceivable to develop the self to become like God if we are not even willing to spend time getting to know Him. We choose to pray and meditate simply because we get to. We get to know God.

Can I change? Yes! Your present personality represents a starting point. The lifestyle behaviors that we discuss in this book are easy to implement. Believers just like you and I frequently change.

A few years ago, we visited a church in which the senior pastor admitted that he failed to spend much time with God. We gradually learned the high frequency with which this occurs--only 6% to 10% of ministers in our research pool spend daily prayer-time with God. As we talked with that minister, he committed to spend time with God on a daily basis. Five months later, he re-assessed himself, but confessed that did

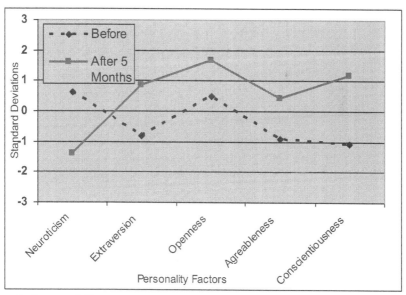

not feel any different. The profile above illustrates the change in that pastor's personality after practicing Listening Prayer once each day for five months.

Can I Change? Yes, try Listening Prayer for just six months. Start by committing to spend time in Listening Prayer just twice each day. You have nothing to lose—everything to gain. The worst thing that can happen is that you will get to know God. However, He might stimulate a change in you.

Can I change? The right question is not, "Can I change, or even, do I want to change?" The right question is, "Do I really want to know God and develop a deeper relationship with Him?" Listening Prayer never serves as a formula to eliminate our dysfunctions or as a means for personal growth. It merely serves as a means of getting to know God and of developing an ever-closer walk with Him. We believers possess an option: Walk continually with God in the Garden of Eden and let the Holy Spirit irrigate our soul, or leave the Garden and its life-changing power. God invites each of us to join Him for a very long walk.

Exercise 19-1: We invite you to complete the following steps:

- For each day of the week, write down how often, how long, and where you will commit to spend time in Listening Prayer. We suggest a minimum of 20 minutes, twice each day as a starting point. Our experience shows that it often takes 17 or 18 minutes to focus totally on God. Although God always remains present, it often takes 17 or 18 minutes before we can mentally focus on Him. Thus, 20 minutes serves as a minimum amount of time to enable a deep connection with God. Note that you may need to select a different time of the day on weekdays than on weekends. Select a location with absolutely no distractions, and then discuss this with your family.

- Write the name of an individual to whom you are willing to make yourself accountable for your commitment. If you feel unwilling to make the commitment to an accountability partner, chances remain extremely remote that you will keep your commitment. Research consistently shows that an accountability partner greatly increases the probability that we will follow through with any new lifestyle behavior. Describe when and how you will contact that person on a regular basis to ensure accountability. If possible, select someone who you normally see on a daily basis.

- Write the names of two to five individuals with whom you want to form a support group. If possible, obtain their commitment to the same process. Nearly every new behavior seems easier to implement when individuals form a support group to discuss and compare mutual experiences about the new behavior. List potential times, places, and durations for meetings. Describe how you will keep the meetings interesting and relevant.

If you have completed the above steps, you are now on a life-long journey of getting to know God. You will never be the same as long as you spend time with Him!

Meditation provides a process of growing into what Thomas a Kempis calls "a familiar friendship with Jesus" (from *The Imitation of Christ)*. Ephesians 4:22-23 says, "You were taught, with regard to your former way of life, to put off your old self, which is being corrupted by its deceitful desires; to be made new in attitude of your minds; and to put on the new self, created to be like God in true righteousness and holiness." The key elements of Ephesians 4:22-23 are:

- Putting off your old self
- Being made new in attitude of your mind
- Putting on the new self
- Becoming more like Him

We hope that you will NOT try to use God by developing new lifestyle behaviors as a way to earn personality change, freedom, or cleansing from dysfunctions. We cannot change our unhealthy motives or eliminate dysfunctions by anything we *do* within ourselves.

The purpose of this lifestyle behavior (Listening Prayer) is simply to get to know God and spend time with Him. As we spend an increasing amount of time with Him, this God of holiness and perfection, He causes change as He convicts each believer, individually. Thus, we gain acceptance only through a personal relationship, and even that is never earned.

For more information on building resilient character traits, please see *Transforming Personality: Spiritual Formation and the Five-Factor Model.* This book represents volume 4 in the Living Well Series outlined on page ii at the front of this book, available in 2013.

REFERENCES

Adler, M. (2001). Conceptualizing and Measuring Appreciation: The development of a new positive psychology construct. *Dissertation Abstracts International, Vol. 63, 08B.*

Babyak, M., J. A. Blumenthal, S. Herman, P. Khatri, P. M. Doraiswamy, K. A. Moore, W. E. Craighead, T. T. Baldewicz, and K. R. Krishnan. (2000). "Exercise treatment for major depression: Maintenance of therapeutic benefit at 10 months." *Psychosomatic Medicine*, 62: 633-638.

Bandura, A. (1986). Social foundations of thought and action: A social cognitive theory. Englewood Cliffs, NJ: Prentice-Hall.

Barbour K.A., T. M. Edenfield, and J. A. Blumenthal. (2007). "Exercise as a treatment for depression and other psychiatric disorders: A review." *Journal of Cardiopulmonary Rehabilitation and Prevention,* 27: 359-367.

Blazer, D. G., Kessler, R. C., McGonagle, K. A., & Swartz, M. S. (1994). The prevalence and distribution of major depression in a national community sample: The National Comorbidity Survey. *American Journal of Psychiatry*, 151, 979-986.

Blumenthal, J. A., M. A. Babyak, K. A. Moore, W. E. Craighead, S. Herman, P. Khatri, R. Waugh, M. A. Napolitano, L. M. Forman, M. Appelbaum, P. M. Doraiswamy, and K. R. Krishnan. "Effects of exercise training on older patients with major depression." *Archives of Internal Medicine*, 159 (1999): 2349-2356.

Blumenthal, J. A., M. A. Babyak, P. M. Doraiswamy, L. Watkins, M. M.

Hoffman, K. A. Barbour, S. Herman, W. E. Craighead, A. L. Brosse, R. Waugh, A. Hinderliter, and A. Sherwood. (2007). "Exercise and pharmacotherapy in the treatment of major depressive disorder." *Psychosomatic Medicine*, 69: 587-596.

Burns, David D. *The Feeling Good Handbook*. New York: Plume: 1999.

Caldwell, M. A., and L. A. Peplau. (1982). "Sex Differences in Same-Sex Friendship.*" Sex Roles*, 8: 721-732.

Chee, M. W. and L. Y Chuah. "Functional Neuroimaging Insights into How Sleep and Sleep Deprivation Affect Memory and Cognition." (2008). *Current Opinions in Neurology*, 21: 417-423.

Christal, R. E (1994). The Air Force Self Description Inventory (AFSDI): Final R&D Status Report. Air Force Research Laboratory, Brooks Air Force Base, San Antonio Texas, November, Metrica, Inc.

Cohen, Gene D., *The Creative Age: Awakening Human Potential in the Second Half of Life*. NY: Harper-Collins, 2000.

Cooper, K. H.. *Faith-Based Fitness*. Nashville, TN: Thomas Nelson Publishers, 2008.

Cosmides, L., and Tooby, J. (1999). Toward an evolutionary taxonomy of treatable conditions. *Journal of Abnormal Psychology*, 108, 453-464.

Davidson, J. C., & Caddell, D. P. (1994). Religion and the meaning of work. *Journal for the Scientific Study of Religion*, 33, 187-202.

Davis, N. W., & Davis, B. J. *Finishing Well: Retirement Skills for Ministers*. North Charleston, SC: CreateSpace, 2012.

Davis, N. W., & Davis, B. J. *Transforming Conflict: Relationship Skills for Ministers*. North Charleston, SC: CreateSpace, 2012.

Davis, N.W., & Davis, B. J. Transforming Personality: Spiritual Formation and the Five-Factor Model. North Charleston, SC: CreateSpace, projected for 2013.

DeVito, Joseph A. *Messages: Building Interpersonal Communication*

Skills. 2nd ed. New York: HarperCollins, 1993.

DeVito, Joseph A. *The Interpersonal Communication Book.* 2nd ed. New York: HarperCollins, 1992.

Egeland, J. A., and A. M. Hostetter. (1990). "Amish Study, I: Affective disorders among the Amish, 1976-1980." *Physiology and Behavior*, 48: 611-616.

Emmons, R.A. *The Psychology of Ultimate Concerns.* New York: Guilford Press, 1999.

Emmons, R.A. & Hill, J. *Words of gratitude for mind, body, and soul.* Radnor, PA: Templeton Foundation Press, 2001.

Emmons, R.A. & Shelton, C.S. (2001). Gratitude and the science of positive psychology. In C.R. Snyder and S.J. Lopez (Eds.), *Handbook of positive psychology.* New York: Oxford University Press.

Emmons, R.A. *The Psychology of Ultimate Concerns.* New York: Guilford Press, 1999.

Emmons, R.A. (2001). Gratitude and mind-body health. *Spirituality and Medicine Connection, 5*, 1-7.

Emmons, R.A. (2003). Acts of gratitude in organizations. In K. S. Cameron, J. E. Dutton, & R. E. Quinn (Eds.), *Positive organizational scholarship* (pp. 81-93). San Francisco: Berrett-Koehler Publishers.

Emmons, R.A., & Crumpler, C.A. (2000). Gratitude as a human strength: Appraising the evidence. *Journal of Social and Clinical Psychology, 19,* 56-69.

Emmons, R.A., & McCullough, M.E. (2003). Counting blessings versus burdens: Experimental studies of gratitude and subjective well-being in daily life. *Journal of Personality and Social Psychology, 84,* 377-389.

Emmons, R.A., Cheung, C., & Tehrani, K. (1998). Assessing spirituality through personal goals: Implications for research on religion and subjective well-being. *Social Indicators Research*, 45, 391-422.

Emmons, R.A., McCullough, M.E., & Tsang, J. (2003). The assessment of gratitude. In S. Lopez & C.R. Snyder (Eds.), *Handbook of positive psychology assessment* (pp. 327-342) Washington, DC: American Psychological Association.

Fehr, Beverley. *Friendship Processes*. Thousand Oaks, CA: Sage Publications, 1996.

Fleming, R., A. Baum, M. M. Gisriel, and R. J. Gathchel, (1982). "Mediating Influences of Social Support at Three Mile Island." *Journal of Human Stress*, 8, no.3, 14-22.

Foster, Richard J. *Celebration of Discipline*, HarperCollins: San Francisco, CA., 1978,

Foster, Richard J., *Celebration of Discipline: The Path to Spiritual Growth*. San Francisco: HarperCollins, 1998.

Gottman, John. *The Seven Principles for Making Marriage Work*. New York: Three Rivers Press, 1999.

Haidt, J. *The Happiness Hypothesis*. New York: Basic Books, 2006.

Hibbeln, J. R. *"Fish Consumption and Major Depression."* Lancet, 351 (1998) 1213.

Holmes, T.H. and Rahe, R.H. (1967). The Social Readjustment Rating Scale. *Journal of Psychosomatic Research,* 11 (2): 213–218.

Ilardi, S. S. The Depression Cure: the 6-step program to beat depression without drugs. DaCapo Press: Cambridge MA., 2009.

Jourard, S. M. Self-disclosure: An Experimental Analysis of the Transparent Self. New York: Wiley-Interscience, 1971.

Kessler, R. C., Berglund, P., Demler, O., Jin, R., & Walters, E. E. (2005). Lifetime prevalence and age-of-onset distributions of DSM-IV disorders in the National Comorbidity Survey replication. *Archives of General Psychiatry*, 62, 593-602.

Lewis, C. S. Mere Christianity. New York: Macmillan, 1960.

Matsushima, Rumi. "The Effect of Hesitancy toward and the Motivation for Self-Disclosure on Loneliness among Japanese Junior High school Students." *Social Behavior and Personality.* (January 2001)

McCullough, M.E., Emmons, R.A., & Tsang, J. (2002). The grateful disposition: A conceptual and empirical topography. *Journal* of Personality and Social Psychology, 82, 112-127.

McCullough, M.E., Kirkpatrick, S., Emmons, R.A., & Larson, D. (2001). Is gratitude a moral affect? *Psychological Bulletin, 127,* 249-266.

Meyer, FP; Canzler, E; Giers, H; Walther, H (1991). "Time course of inhibition of caffeine elimination in response to the oral depot contraceptive agent Deposiston. Hormonal contraceptives and caffeine elimination". *Zentralbl Gynakol* **113** (6): 297–302. PMID 2058339.

Miller, L. C., and J. H. Berg, J. H. "Selectivity and Urgency in Interpersonal Exchange." In *Communication, Intimacy and Close Relationships*, edited by V. J. Derlega, 161-205. Orlando, FL: Academic Press, 1984.

National Sleep Foundation. *2008 Sleep in America Poll* (2008).

Ortweiler, W; Simon, HU; Splinter, FK; Peiker, G; Siegert, C; Traeger, A (1985). "Determination of caffeine and metamizole elimination in pregnancy and after delivery as an in vivo method for characterization of various cytochrome p-450 dependent biotransformation reactions". *Biomed Biochim Acta.* **44** (7–8): 1189–99. PMID 4084271.

Peet, M. and D. F. Horrobin. "A Dose-Ranging Study of the Effects of Ethyl-Eicosapentaenoate in Patients with Ongoing Depression Despite Apparently Adequate Treatment with Standard Drugs." Archives of General Psychiatry, 59 (2002): 913-919.

Peet, M., B.Murphy, J. Shay, and D. Horrobin. "Depletion of Omega-3 Fatty Acid Levels in Red Blood Cell Membranes of Depressive Patients." *Biological Psychiatry*, 43 (1998): 315-319.

Penedo, F. J. and J. R. Dahn, (2005) "Exercise and well-being: A review of mental and physical health benefits associated with physical activity." *Current Opinion in Psychiatry*, 18: 189-193.

Pennebaker, J. W., J. K. Kiecolt-Glaser, and T. Glaser. "Disclosure of Traumas and Immune Function: Health Implications of Psychotherapy." *Journal of Consulting and Clinical Psychology* 56 (1988): 239-245.

Peterson, C. *A primer in positive psychology*. Oxford University Press: New York, 2006.

Peterson, C., Park, N., & Seligman, M. E. P. (2006). Strengths of character and recovery. *Journal of Positive Psychology* 1.

Piper, W. (1989). The little engine that could. New York: Platt and Monk. (Original work published in 1930)

Pollan, M. In Defense of Food: An Eater's Manifesto. New York: Penguin Press, 2008.

Rechtschaffen, A., B. M. Bergmann, C. A. Everson, C. A. Kushida, and M. A. Gilliland. (2002). "Sleep Deprivation in the Rat: X. Integration and Discussion of the Findings. 1989." *Sleep*, 25: 68-87.

Rowell, Jeren L. (2010). Ministerial Attrition: When Clergy Call It Quits: The Relationship of Superintendents and Pastors, ANSR Conference, March 25, 2010.

Ryan, R. M., Sheldon, K. M., Kasser, T., & Deci, E., L. (1996). All goals are not created equal: An organismic perspective on the nature of goals and their regulation. In P. M. Gollwitzer & J. A. Bargh (Eds), *The psychology of action: Linking cognition and motivation to behavior* (pp. 7-26). New York: Guilford Press.

Schiraldi, Glenn R. *Building Self-Esteem: A 125 Day Program*. Ellicott City MD: Chevron Publishing Corp., 1993.

Seigman, M. E. P. (2002). *Authentic Happiness*. New York: Free Press.

Seligman, M. E. P. (1990). Why is there so much depression today? The waxing of the individual and the waning of the commons. In R. E. Ingram (Ed.), *Contemporary psychological approaches to depression* (pp. 1-9). New York: Plenum.

Snyder C. R., & Lopez S. J. *The Handbook of Positive Psychology*, New York: Oxford University Press, 2002.

Snyder, C. R. *Handbook of Hope: Theory, Measures, & Applications*. San Diego, CA: Academic Press, 2000.

Sundquist, K., Frank, G., & Sundquist, J. (2004). Urbanization and incidence of psychosis and depression. *British Journal of Psychiatry*, 184, 293-298.

Sundquist, K., Frank, G., & Sundquist, J. (2004). Urbanization and incidence of psychosis and depression. *British Journal of Psychiatry*, 184, 293-298.

Taylor, D. A., and I. Altman (1966). "Intimacy-scaled stimuli for use in studies of interpersonal relations." *Psychological Reports*, 19, 729-730.

Templeton, J. M. Worldwide laws of life: 200 eternal spiritual principles. Radnor, PA: Templeton Press, 1997.

Tupes, E. C., & Christal, R. E. (1992). Recurrent personality factors based on trait ratings. *Journal of Personality*, 60 (2), 223-251.

U.S. Department of Health and Human Services. Physical Activity and Health: A report of the Surgeon General. Atlanta: U.S. Department of Health and Human Services, Centers for Disease Control and Prevention National Center for Chronic Disease Prevention and Health Promotion, 1999.

Van Boven, L., and Gilovich, T., (2003). To Do or To Have? That Is the Question. *Journal of Personality and Social Psychology*. Vol. 85, No. 6, 1193-1202.

Worthington, E. L., Jr. (2005). Five steps to forgiveness: The art and science of forgiving. New York: Crown House.

Wood, George O. *A Psalm in Your Heart*, Gospel Publishing House:

Springfield MO, 2002.

Yancey, Phillip. *What's So Amazing About Grace?* Zondervan: 2002.

Answer to exercise on page 6—

Villagers were getting hurt who never needed to get hurt.

Likewise, ministers who never need to succumb to burnout sometimes martyr themselves by burnout.

ABOUT THE AUTHORS

Nathan Davis
Beth Davis

In her primary role as Director of HealthCare Ministries, Beth leads teams that provide healthcare and medical resources world-wide. She is a board certified health care chaplain with a Doctor of Ministry degree. Prior to her marriage to Nathan, Beth served for 25 years as a missionary in Vietnam, the Philippines, Hong Kong, and Belgium.

Nathan grew up in Japan, the son of missionaries Dr. Jim and Genevieve Davis. Before becoming a missionary, Nathan served the US Air Force as a psychologist for 29 years. Nathan's primary role is facilitating seminars on relationship enhancement skills, crisis debriefing skills, spiritual formation, burnout prevention skills, stress management, and retirement transition issues. In the process of teaching preventative skills, Nathan and Beth consult each year those who seek confidential pastoral counseling on issues such as depression, anxiety, transition issues, marital stress, and conflict resolution.

Made in the USA
Charleston, SC
15 August 2012